If this book has landed in your hands, it's probably here for a reason.
If it's not your thing, do me a favour and leave it somewhere public so it can find someone who needs it more.
And if you're reading this and genuinely want to study it but money's tight, my contact details are in the back. Reach out — I'll send you a copy for free.

It's You. Oh Fuck. It's ME.

A Therapist's View on Relationships.

Chad Taylor

Copyright

Published independently by Chad Taylor

First edition, 2026

ISBN: 978-1-7644769-0-4

Printed Worldwide

Dedication

For Sophie.

For my daughters, Madi and Zoe.

For Ted.

For my parents.

For everyone.

Author's Note

This is the book I didn't know I needed.

This book wasn't planned. It wasn't strategic. At the price of around two fucking coffees, it definitely wasn't written to make me rich. And I haven't published it because I thought the world needed another book about relationships. It exists because at some point I realised I was living proof of the problem I kept blaming everyone else for.

After enough failed relationships, two of them giving me my daughters, I hit a wall. Not dramatically. Not with fireworks. Just the slow, familiar realisation that I was repeating the same shit with different people and calling it bad luck.

I was the epitome of "it's you." I wore being a victim like a fucking badge of honour. My upbringing didn't help, but I took that excuse and ran with it. I almost turned victimhood into an Olympic sport.

This behaviour grew out of being spoiled by my aunts and uncles. The worse I described how things were at home, the more I was spoilt. This wasn't intentional, but this was my programming. "Poor me" earned me lollies, chocolate and outings, and I learned that this was a currency of love.

Because this worked so well, I mistook oversharing for intimacy. I learned how to make people feel sorry for me and called it "being open". I didn't just do it with partners. I did it everywhere. It was how I got validation without actually being vulnerable. Oversharing and vulnerability are two very different things, and I found out the fucking hard way.

From the outside, I looked fine. Successful enough. Comfortable. Owned my own home early. Had more toys than I needed. On paper, I was winning. But whenever things didn't go my way, I defaulted straight back to victim mode. It was my emotional love language. Blame outward, relief inward.

After leaving yet another relationship abruptly, I met a man who changed my life. Not because he gave me answers, but because he dismantled the unconscious belief I'd been running on my entire life. I didn't wake up one morning and suddenly realise "oh fuck, I'm the problem". It took years. Therapy. Study. Reading. Brutal self-searching. Being told shit I didn't want to hear and couldn't unhear once I had. That man was Ted. He came in and out of my life at exactly the right times. He woke me up without me knowing I was asleep. Much of what you'll read in this book comes straight out of the notebooks I filled during my studies and the hours I spent in therapy with him. Ted told me more than once to "write the book".

So here it is.

Thank you to Jenny, Ted's partner. The time and presence you gave me mattered more than you probably realise.

Thank you to the sangha I was part of during that time. Every one of you helped me see parts of myself I couldn't access alone. I hope you're all still growing, still questioning, still uncomfortable enough to stay awake.

My parents, thank you for showing me how I don't want to be in relationships. No bitterness. No resentment. I love you both today for who you are, not who I wish you were. We all do the best we can from our level of consciousness and the information available to us.

My daughters, Madi and Zoe. You're the reason I'm still alive and writing this book. There were times I wanted to check out completely, but I couldn't do that to you. You challenge the fuck out of me in very different ways, and because of that, you force me to grow every single day.

Alcoholics Anonymous, the most honest way of life I've ever encountered. It's a shame most of us don't arrive there until we're completely fucked. The 12 Steps, when applied beyond alcohol and drugs, are a blueprint for living consciously. Without AA, I'm fucked. Drunk or sober.

Bruce, my sponsor for many years, I miss you every day.

My previous partners, even though things didn't work out, you played a role in waking me up. Even though I don't think any of you would say I was a cunt, I also wasn't the man I am today. If you still carry hurt from our time together, I am genuinely sorry for the ways I contributed to that. If you're reading this instead of burning it, I'm open to making further amends. Every one of those relationships shaped me. For that, I'm grateful.

My therapy clients and my AA sponsees, I'm deeply aware of the privilege it is to sit with you in your lives. Half the time I wonder who's really paying who.

Rod, my therapist, you're a fucking legend. It took me a while to relax when you called me darling, but the growth has been undeniable.

Dean, my co-host on the Conversations for Conscious Relationships podcast. It's great to share the journey with you, brother.

Metavision Institute and my university cohort, especially Claire: without you, this book doesn't get written. When we met at uni I didn't even know how to structure an essay. Your guidance, friendship, and brutal honesty shaped this book more than you know.

David and Victoria, my supervisors, chosen deliberately for very different reasons. One to sharpen my clinical edge. The other to remind me of the spiritual wisdom we've lost along the way.

And last, but definitely not least, Sophie Roya, my amazing partner. Without a relationship with you, this book is just theory. You've shown me that two people, both flawed in their own ways, can come together and create something deeply connected and real. The way you hold yourself and show up in our relationship constantly amazes me. I still catch myself pinching myself at how we connect, the life we've built, and the way we handle disagreements and misunderstandings. Not perfectly, but honestly.

I've learned that we only ever have the day we're in. Life happens in moments, not guarantees, and I want many more of those moments with you. I choose you the same way I choose sobriety, one day at a time. Not because I have to. Because I want to. Each day I choose to love you to the best of my ability and do the next right thing. To be together because we choose to, not because we have to.

Without you, this book doesn't exist. It's that simple. On top of the relationship journey I share with you, the hours of help you have given me couldn't have been more thorough.

Starting our couples retreats and podcast together, and taking this work to the world with you, is an honour. You have so much to share with the world.

Introduction

What's actually failing in relationships?

I could sum this book up in one line:

Relationships fail because we are unconscious of our own shit.

As a clinical psychotherapist, not a conventional one though, the pattern I see over and over again isn't lack of love, communication skills, or effort. It's unawareness. Unawareness looks like blame. Projection. Externalising our own unresolved shit onto the person closest to us.

How do I know this? Because I'm human. I fight the same instincts you do. The only difference now is I'm aware of what's happening, and even that doesn't magically fix it. Knowing isn't enough. We all know we should eat better, exercise more, sleep properly. Knowledge without practice does fuck all. I can sit in a garage making engine noises all day; I'm still not a car.

The theory matters. But the experience is what changes us.

Working on myself, and now with thousands of clients, I've watched the same moment happen again and again. That quiet, uncomfortable realisation:

"Oh fuck... it's me."

Once that lands, the real work can begin.

This book is for people who want to be better. Better partners. Better lovers. Better parents. Better friends. It's for people who already sense they're acting like an arsehole sometimes but don't know why. It feels like being hijacked. Like something else takes the wheel. And it does, just not anything mystical or external. It's something far deeper and far more human than that.

I don't believe we're born fucked. I believe we're never taught how to live consciously.

This book is my attempt to explain what happened to us along the way, and why without doing the work we keep repeating the same relationship patterns while blaming the wrong person. I'm not a guru. I'm not selling salvation. What you're reading is raw, lived experience, moving from disharmony toward harmony in my own life and helping others do the same.

If you're reading this, part of you is already thinking about replacing your partner to fix things. Sorry, you're not wrong, but you're not right either. Wake up. You're part of the problem too.

This book isn't written in a conventional structure. I wrote it for me. It's the book I needed, but couldn't find. If you get something out of it, great. If not, it's still done its job by showing me where I need to keep growing.

Humour matters here. Sometimes the only way through deep shit is to laugh at ourselves. Over time, that's where real change starts.

I was once told: If you want to learn something, teach it. Thanks Ted. That's why this book exists.

What follows is simple:
What life was like.
What happened.
And what it's like now.

Nothing here is new. I've just pulled the threads together and told the truth as cleanly as I know how.

I will attempt to use the best format I know:
Problem.
Solution.
Action.

I'm sure he never invented it, but thanks to Bill Wilson for the learning model that has worked best for me.

To the professional critic, my audience is the person that wouldn't normally pick up a book like this. I will be happy for your feedback, I always love to see where I can do better, but the main objective was to reach people — even one person — who may have never gotten the chance to "wake up".

If you're uncomfortable already, good. You're exactly where you need to be. If you're not, it would be great if you could pay it forward. Give it away or leave it somewhere to be picked up. I trust the book will get to those that it's meant for.

How To Read This Book

This isn't a book to smash through on a Sunday afternoon so you can say you've "done the work". If that's your plan, you'll miss it. Read this slowly. Not because the words are hard, but because you might be. Some of this will land. Some of it will piss you off. Some of it will feel uncomfortably familiar. That's the point.

If you find yourself wanting to rush, skim, or jump ahead to the "fix", then pause. That impulse is the same one that probably shows up in your relationships. This book isn't asking you to be perfect. It's asking you to notice.

You don't need to agree with everything here. You don't need to like me. You definitely don't need to turn this into another self improvement project. Read a chapter. Put it down. Let it stir shit up. Notice what you defend against, what you soften around, and what you want to argue with. That's where the real work is.

Some chapters are short. Some will hit harder than others. You might read one in ten minutes and then sit with it for an hour. Good. That's not falling behind, that's actually reading.

And one last thing. This book won't save your relationship, fix your partner, or give you a shiny new identity. If you're looking for that, you've got the wrong book. What it can do is help you see yourself more clearly. And from there, everything else changes. With that said, let's start where most of us went wrong without ever realising it.

Contents

Chapter 1

"It's You": Blame Culture is Fucking Relationships

The Empty Boat by Thích Nhất Hạnh

"A monk decides to meditate alone. Away from his monastery, he takes a boat and goes to the middle of the lake, closes his eyes and begins to meditate.

After a few hours of unperturbed silence, he suddenly feels the blow of another boat hitting his. With his eyes still closed, he feels his anger rising and, when he opens his eyes, he is ready to shout at the boatman who dared to disturb his meditation. But when he opened his eyes, saw that it was an empty boat, not tied up, floating in the middle of the lake...

At that moment, the monk achieves self realisation and understands that anger is within him; it simply needs to hit an external object to provoke it.

After that, whenever he meets someone who irritates or provokes his anger, he remembers; the other person is just an empty boat.

Anger is inside me."

***

Projection, blame, and externalisation hijack relationships. Most people don't think of themselves as blaming types. Blame sounds harsh. Obvious. Something other people do. But blame is rarely loud. It's usually quiet, convincing, and dressed up as logic, righteousness, or "just being honest". It's also one of the most effective ways to avoid genuine contact with others and with ourselves. This isn't a modern problem. We didn't invent it with Instagram, Twitter, or therapy language. We just industrialised it.

Blame culture, what's that? Our minds are trained for one thing in relationships: "You're the fucking problem". Not in a way that shows "I've looked openly at why I think that", we aren't that aware. More like the way an alcoholic explains why everyone else is the cause of their drinking. It's always convincing. At least to us. We externalise or project onto others what we haven't healed in ourselves. Simple, hey?

This is projection in its rawest form. It's not malicious. It's protective. It's the psyche saying, "If I can keep this over there, I don't have to feel it in here". With the internet, social media, and endless ways to judge the world, we're set up to feel superior. We're trapped inside 'our' way of thinking more than ever. We don't just have opinions anymore. We have identities built around them. And the more we identify, the harder it becomes to see clearly.

Being "right" is a fucking drug. Look at the epidemic levels of polarity in the world. And the most insane part is it's the same inside our own psyche. Ever been in a conversation with someone who holds an opposing view on something that actually matters to you? You're biting your gum to pieces, swallowing what you want to say, doing everything you can not to lose your shit. Well done if you manage to not turn into a complete fuckwit. But now it poisons you from the inside while giving you another enemy to fight in your head. Feels good though, doesn't it? That justified anger.

Partner. Kids. Boss. Pick a target. The slow driver who held you up. The fast idiot who overtook you. The mind doesn't care. This is where relationships quietly rot. Not in screaming matches, but in swallowed words, rehearsed arguments, and imagined victories.

Justified anger is one of the most addictive emotional states there is. It makes us feel powerful. Superior. Right. Because as long as they're the problem, you don't have to look at yourself. Anger gives direction. Blame gives certainty. And certainty feels a lot safer than not knowing who the fuck you are without the story.

The craziest part? Most of us think we're being reasonable. Hook us up to a lie detector and we'd probably pass. We think we're communicating. We think we're setting boundaries. We think we're self aware. Half the time we're just using therapy language as a weapon to defend our identity, defending it to the death from the idea that we might be part of the problem.

Self awareness has become performative. Insight has become armour. And language, once meant to connect, has become a shield. As long as the focus stays on everyone and everything else, you're safe. Safe from what? Self reflection. Responsibility. Growing the fuck up.

Blame doesn't just distance you from others. It distances you from adulthood. You cannot be deeply connected to someone you believe is broken, beneath you, or "the one who needs fixing". I was once told after a breakup, "Next time you find a partner, use consciousness. If you can't accept them exactly as they are, go buy an old car and do that up. A partner isn't a project".

Superiority kills intimacy faster than betrayal ever could. The more morally superior you feel, the more unconscious you become. And let's be honest, how much do we really fucking know? Scientists once would've died defending the belief that the universe was 99.9% matter. Quantum mechanics blew that to pieces.

Certainty ages badly. Humility evolves. Closed mindedness isn't a lack of intelligence, it's fear. Fear convincing you of its certainty. We won't dare question our position because that would mean uncertainty, vulnerability, or responsibility. Responsibility feels unbearable when your whole identity is built on not being at fault. Blame promises safety. Responsibility threatens collapse.

Look at the modern world, social media, outrage culture, therapy speak. It almost looks like we wake up each day asking, "Where can I assert my dominance?". We are drowning in confirmation that our view is correct. ChatGPT, Gemini or Grok, these AI cunts have poured petrol on being right. They're designed to make you feel invincible. When I asked one to check grammar, it told me I wasn't writing a book, I was writing a reckoning. We'll see.

Being right has never been easier. Being honest has never been harder. We aren't more open minded than previous generations, we're more entrenched. More polarised. More convinced that anyone who disagrees with us is unconscious, abusive, toxic, narcissistic, or "hasn't done the work". Like we can fucking talk.

Projection doesn't disappear with education. Sometimes it just gets better vocabulary. We polarise everything: right and wrong, good and bad, victim and perpetrator, conscious and unconscious. And conveniently, we always land on the "right" side of the divide. The egocentricity loves moral high ground. It's a great place to avoid being seen.

Relationships get absolutely fucked here. Intimacy cannot survive moral superiority. It just can't. If everyone you get close to eventually becomes the problem, the common denominator isn't bad luck. If one person thinks you're a dickhead, it could go either way. If everyone thinks you're a dickhead, wipe the window. It's a mirror. That mirror is the one most of us avoid at all costs. The common denominator is you.

So what happens when blame stops working? Here's the truth. The only real answer to unconscious projection is conscious recollection, turning the finger back toward yourself instead of firing it outward. It's the moment blame collapses and responsibility starts, not in a moral way, but in a grown the fuck up way. Instead of "what's wrong with you?", the question becomes "what the hell is this waking up in me?". Most people never get here because it's destabilising and strips the egocentricity of its favourite toys. We're not doing that work yet. That comes later. For now, just know this. Projection is automatic, recollection is earned, and everything in this book is slowly moving you toward that turn.

Awakening doesn't start with insight. It starts with collapse. And when collapse hits, we do what we've always done.

Most people don't get curious, they get uncomfortable. The story cracks. The certainty drops out. And what's left isn't clarity, it's sensation. Tight chest. Restlessness. Anxiety. A low level panic that something is wrong but you don't know what. The nervous system doesn't experience that as an invitation to grow, it experiences it as a threat. So it does what it's always done. It looks for relief. It looks for control. It looks for a way out.

We escape.

Chapter 2

Escapism: (or what looks like escapism)

The Mexican Fisherman

"An American investment banker was taking a much-needed vacation in a small coastal Mexican village when a small boat with just one fisherman docked. The boat had several large, fresh fish in it. The investment banker was impressed by the quality of the fish and asked the Mexican how long it took to catch them.

The Mexican replied, "Only a little while". The banker then asked why he didn't stay out longer and catch more fish. The Mexican fisherman replied he had enough to support his family's immediate needs.

The American then asked, "But what do you do with the rest of your time?"

The Mexican fisherman replied, "I sleep late, fish a little, play with my children, take siesta with my wife, stroll into the village each evening where I sip wine and play guitar with my amigos: I have a full and busy life, señor."

The investment banker scoffed, "I am an Ivy League MBA, and I could help you. You could spend more time fishing and with the proceeds buy a bigger boat, and with the proceeds from the bigger boat, you could buy several boats until eventually, you would have a whole fleet of fishing boats. Instead of selling your catch to the middleman you could sell directly to the processor, eventually opening your own cannery. You could control the product, processing and distribution." Then he added, "Of course, you would need to leave this small coastal fishing village and move to Mexico City where you would run your growing enterprise."

The Mexican fisherman asked, "But señor, how long will this all take?"

To which the American replied, "15–20 years."

"But what then?" asked the Mexican.

The American laughed and said, "That's the best part. When the time is right you would announce an IPO and sell your company stock to the public and become very rich. You could make millions."

"Millions, señor? Then what?"

To which the investment banker replied, "Then you would retire. You could move to a small coastal fishing village where you would sleep late, fish a little, play with your kids, take siesta with your wife, stroll to the village in the evenings where you could sip wine and play your guitar with your amigos."

***

We will do anything to avoid looking at ourselves. We chase relief. We chase control, having no fucking idea it's because we feel completely out of control. We chase something outside ourselves to fix an internal problem. We don't have "insecurity". We have a lack of inner security. This isn't a moral failing. It's a strategy - an unconscious one. A way of managing what we don't know how to sit with.

So we trade our partners in for younger, hotter models and do insane shit in the name of a high. Have we ever actually stopped and asked ourselves what the fuck we're doing? Big cars. Big careers. Fancy clothes. Oversized houses. Hot partners. Alcohol. Cocaine. Porn. Sex. Scrolling. Work. Gym. It all looks great from the outside. Inside it's chaotic, restless, irritable, discontented. It's never enough. Ever.

We call this choice. We call it freedom. We tell ourselves a story that makes it all feel intentional. I'm choosing this. I want this. I need this. If I just get this, everything will finally be worthwhile. But most of the time we're not choosing, we're escaping. Escaping discomfort. Emptiness. Anxiety. Depression. And the fucked part? We don't know we're doing it.

It's like driving flat out down a highway in a station wagon. Every emotion, memory, and experience we should've dealt with gets tossed into the back like McDonald's wrappers. If we just keep fucking driving, we never have to look.

We drink to feel relaxed.
We work to feel worthy.
We fuck to feel wanted.
We buy to feel important.
We chase novelty to feel alive.

Worst of all, we bail on relationships to feel 'free' again. And for a moment, it works. Just long enough to convince us it's the solution. Until the honeymoon ends, the dopamine drops, and the same patterns show up wearing a different mask. We don't have multiple partners, we just switch out the leading actor or actress. And somehow we still believe we're not the problem. This is where dopamine quietly takes over. Dopamine doesn't give a shit about meaning or intimacy. It only cares about pursuit, excitement, and reward.

New job.
New partner.
New house.
New city.
New gym.
New kink.
New identity.

Fuck yeah. Look at me go. See? I'm not the problem. Every obsession starts with a rush. Like a drug. Because it is a drug. I have no moral high ground here, I've chased highs my whole life. But when the buzz fades, what's left is you. And whatever you were avoiding before the high kicked in. This book is a bit like that, Sophie's asking regularly, "Why the rush?". Exactly. When dopamine drops, the nervous system panics. And instead of staying and getting conscious, we blow shit up.

I chose the wrong partner.
This relationship is holding me back.
She's this. He's that.
I need my freedom.

Sounds empowered. Usually it's fear in fucking disguise. Anything you use compulsively to dodge your own shit owns you. This is why the word addiction makes people defensive. Most people hear "addiction" and think of rock bottom. Rehab. AA. The bloke in the park with a brown paper bag. But addiction isn't about substances, it's about relief. Workaholism. Sex. Porn. Spirituality. Self-help. Fitness. Money. Achievement. Relationships themselves. Doesn't matter what the thing is, it's the same pattern.

Twenty-four years in AA and I've seen every version of transference there is. We don't stop escaping, we just swap vehicles. And the world doesn't just allow this behaviour, it rewards it.

We live in a culture of getting through this moment so we can reach the next one, because maybe that one will save us. What the fuck do we even think salvation looks like? Would we recognise it if it punched us in the face?

The real problem is we worship this behaviour. Every second cunt on Instagram thinks they're an entrepreneur because they ticked a box. We call this success. Aspirational. Something to "get to". Nobody questions it. We've normalised dysfunction and called it ambition. This is escapism dressed up as a lifestyle. An instinctual drive for safety, worth, and connection met in the clumsiest way possible. And until we stop running, we'll keep calling escape "freedom", and wondering why we still feel empty when we get there.

We don't escape because we're broken. We escape because we can't sit with what's moving inside us. Sensations, emotions, and instincts doing their job. Until we learn how to feel instead of flee, we'll keep repeating the same shit and call it "choice".

Chapter 3

Emotions, Instincts, and Why We Fuck Up

Viktor Frankl

"When a person can't find a deep sense of meaning, they distract themselves with pleasure."

Carl Jung

"Until you make the unconscious conscious, it will direct your life and you will call it fate."

Erich Fromm

"Man is the only animal for whom his own existence is a problem which he has to solve."

***

This chapter isn't about fixing you. It's about showing you why willpower keeps failing.

So what actually is an emotion? Energy in motion. That's it. Not mystical. Not complicated. Just energy moving through the body and informing the mind. And yet most of us were taught very early not to fucking have them.

"Deal with it."
"Calm down."
"Stop crying."
"Don't be angry."

Usually because our emotions inconvenienced the adults around us. "Don't be angry near me, now I'm angry that you're angry". So from the start, emotions aren't welcomed. They're managed, silenced, corrected, or shamed. And then we act surprised when people yell, punch things, smash shit, or implode relationships. Why does a teenager lose their mind and break their fist on a brick wall? Because the energy inside them has nowhere to go. When energy can't move through, it goes out. That's projection. Other people become the screen. We're the projector.

This is why we dump shit on our partners, our kids, our bosses, strangers on the internet. It's not because we're evil. It's because the system is overloaded and looking for a release valve. Now add instincts to the mix, and this is where we really fuck things up.

Our three main instinctual drives are Sex, Security, and Social Connection.

We like to pretend we're above this, but we're not. These drives kept us alive as a species. Without them, we'd be extinct.

If there wasn't an orgasm at the end, how many of us would chase sex like we do? PornHub wouldn't be a billion dollar company, that's for sure.

Instincts aren't the problem. Blind instincts are. Obsessed instincts are. These systems are ancient. They don't give a shit about intimacy, long term love, or conscious relating. They care about survival, status, and getting needs met now.

So when we're triggered, instincts hijack us. We become jealous. Territorial. Needy. Avoidant. Controlling. Desperate. Not because we're broken, but because the old brain is driving. This isn't personal failure. It's biology running outdated software in a modern world.

And here's the bit we hate admitting: humans are not special. Every animal on the planet is wired the same way. Survive. Reproduce. Belong. The difference? Animals don't dress it up as "communication issues" or "relationship values". They just follow the impulse. We wrap ours in stories and call it morality, logic, or identity. That's where our arrogance kicks in.

We separate ourselves from nature, as if we're above it. That's how fucking narcissistic we are as humans. We have 'nature' and we have 'human nature', as if we're not animals too. We share 50% of our DNA with a tree, for fuck's sake. About 65% with chickens. Around 88% with dolphins. And 98.99% with a chimpanzee.

We claim 'human nature' and 'nature'. No. Same fucking thing.

Ever seen a male dog go feral when a female is on heat? That instinct takes over completely. Should we punish him for it? We do, because it inconveniences us. Ever watched zebras crossing a river? The safest place is the middle of the herd. That's the security instinct in action. Smart as fuck. Chimpanzees? They've got dominance hierarchies, submission signals, and reconciliation rituals: grooming, contact, repair. How's your repair ritual - do you even know what these fucking words mean; does it even exist? Mine used to be absolute shit.

So before we talk solutions, we need to understand what actually happens inside us. Here's the Chad two minute version of the brain. The human brain evolved in three rough layers:

The back brain, brainstem / reptilian brain.
Breathing. Heart rate. Survival reflexes. Fight. Flight. Freeze. Fawn.

The middle brain, mammalian.
Where most instincts live. Emotion, attachment, threat detection.

The front brain, the neocortex.
This is where reflection happens. Regulation. Choice. Empa-

happens. Regulation. Choice. Empathy. Thinking before speaking.
This is the part we think is running the show.

Now here's the problem. When we're triggered, emotionally activated, we lose access to the front brain. It goes functionally offline. And this is why we fuck up. The lights are on, but nobody's home. At least nobody capable of nuance, kindness, or shutting the fuck up.

And plenty of things weaken the front brain even before conflict shows up. Stress. Social media. Porn. Gambling. Exhaustion. Love. But the biggest contributor? Drugs and alcohol.

Make sense now why your partner watched porn after a few wines?
Why they sent a nude to a coworker?
Why you said something nuclear you "didn't mean"?
Why you woke up next to someone you wouldn't normally choose?

Front brain offline. Instincts in charge.

The same thing happens when two people's instincts collide. No one is thinking clearly. Everyone is defending. Both people are convinced they are right.

You can stay conscious, but it takes effort.
Awareness.
Humility.
Practice.
And people around you willing to do the same.

And let's be honest, we are always in collision with someone. There are over eight billion of us now. You are not escaping this.

If you've ever lost your shit, and of course you have, this is a massive reason anxiety and depression show up. A chronic instinct hijack without understanding or regulation burns the system out.

When we don't understand what's happening underneath, in the body, in the nervous system, in our need for safety and connection, the fallout isn't freedom. It's anxiety. It's numbness. It's depression. Not because something's wrong with us, but because something vital is being missed.

Chapter 4

Anxiety, Depression, and the Search For Connection (what the GP didn't fucking explain)

Buddha

"Do not dwell in the past, do not dream of the future, concentrate the mind on the present moment."

Seneca (Roman Stoic)

"Life is very short and anxious for those who forget the past, neglect the present, and fear the future."

Mark Epstein

"The present moment is often intolerable when we are at war with our inner life."

Eckhart Tolle

"Time isn't precious at all, because it is an illusion."
"Psychological time is the primary cause of suffering."

***

At some point, usually without realising it, something shifts. It could come as a result of a large event, but can sometimes just be a slow burn. Life doesn't feel wrong exactly. It just feels off. You're functioning. Working. Parenting. Fucking. Scrolling. Drinking. Coping. From the outside, it looks fine. From the inside, there's tension, flatness, noise that never really shuts the fuck up. That's usually when the question appears: What the fuck is wrong with me? And that's where anxiety and depression quietly walk in.

We live in a world where mental health is completely fucked. A quick look at the stats tells the story. One in four people in the Western world has a registered mental health diagnosis. That doesn't include the people who've never seen a doctor, or the millions, maybe billions, medicating in other ways. And no, I don't just mean drugs and alcohol. Porn has now overtaken substance use statistically. Let that sink in. Gambling is at epidemic levels. We have hundreds of 12 Step support groups, for every obsession we can fucking think of. One of the latest additions, ITAA, is a 12 Step fellowship for internet and technology addiction.

So what aren't we being taught? The simple explanation:

Anxiety is the mind disconnected and projected into the future. Depression is the mind disconnected and stuck in the past. That's it. Be nice if the medical model could say it that clearly. Instead it's usually: get you in, label you, medicate you, get you out. But look at the pattern.

Anxiety lives in what might happen.
Depression lives in what already happened.
Both drag us out of the present moment.

And here's the part we completely miss. The present moment isn't some wanky spiritual concept. It's where the body lives. Thinking lives in time, past and future. Feeling lives now. The real problem is almost always the same: we're living in our heads and leaving our bodies behind. We are living in dualistic thinking. Dualistic thinking is best described as "this or that" thinking. Not "both and" thinking. Mind or body. Thinking or feeling. Expansion or contraction. Sun or rain. Black or white. Good or bad. Mine or yours.

We really need to move into a state of non-dualistic thinking. Mind and body. Thinking and feeling. Expansion and contraction. Sun and rain. Black and white. Good and bad. Mine and yours. The truth is, we are both the mind, and the body. We think and we feel. Things expand and contract. It can rain while it's sunny. Everything lives in a fucking shade of grey (some more black, some more white). Things can be good and bad at the same time, depending on who's fucking looking and what the topic is. And lastly, in a relationship, everything is mine and yours. In other words, 'ours'.

Now here's where I part ways in my thinking with a lot of people. I don't actually believe we're trying to escape with our maladaptive behaviours discussed in the previous chapter, even though that's what it looks like. I think we're trying to get back to the present moment and feel whole again. In other words, we're trying to go in, we just don't fucking know it.

These behaviours are unconscious attempts to reconnect. To feel peace. To feel okay inside our own skin. Connected is what we're chasing. Not escape. The tragedy is we confuse short term relief with real connection. So we scroll. Drink. Fuck. Buy. Work. Obsess. Meditate like it's a productivity tool. And even when it stops working, we keep doing it, or we just swap it for something else. Honestly, how many times do you get up from scrolling and feel better? Exactly. The very things we reach for to feel okay end up maintaining the problem. Sometimes they make it worse.

Anxiety and depression aren't signs that you're broken. They're signals. Signals that the nervous system has been living in tension, instinct, and avoidance for too long without a way to settle, feel, or reconnect. The system never gets to complete the cycle. And before we start talking about fixing relationships, intimacy, or sex, this has to be understood. Otherwise we just keep treating symptoms, getting stuck on the merry-go-round, and wondering why nothing actually changes. Now, before you jump down my throat, here's the disclaimer. I am not saying medication, hospitalisation, or professional intervention aren't needed. If that were true, I wouldn't be alive to write this book.

I've had shock therapy.
A shitload of prescriptions.
Mental health ward admissions.
Endless therapy.
Thousands of AA meetings.

I believe we should all be in therapy for the duration of our lives. That used to be normal. It was built into tribal living. There was always a shaman, medicine woman, priest, or other healer outside of the family that we went to regularly.

What I am saying is this: medication without understanding disconnection just manages the noise. It doesn't explain or resolve the signal. We need to start treating the cause, not the symptom. And if we don't understand the signal, we'll keep searching for connection in all the wrong fucking places.

Chapter 5

False Connection (why it feels good, why it's bullshit, and why it never lasts)

Sigmund Freud

"It is that we are never so defenceless against suffering as when we love, never so helplessly unhappy as when we have lost our loved object or its love."

Carl Jung

"People will do anything, no matter how absurd, to avoid facing their own soul."

Will Rogers

"We buy things we don't need with money we don't have to impress people we don't like."

***

False connection survives because it gives you just enough to keep you from facing the truth. Just enough warmth to not freeze. Just enough dopamine to not feel dead. Just enough distraction to avoid asking the question that would actually change your life. That question isn't "what's wrong with my partner?". It's "why can't I sit still with myself without reaching for something?".

False connection thrives on speed. Quick hits. Short circuits. It hates silence. It hates pauses. It hates moments where you might actually feel the loneliness underneath the behaviour instead of medicating it. That's why scrolling feels unbearable when you stop. That's why the gym turns into obsession. That's why sex turns into performance. That's why spirituality turns into bypassing. Anything but stillness. Anything but feeling. Take the social media apps off your phone and watch yourself pull the phone out of your pocket again, staring stupidly at it wondering why the fuck you just got it out.

And here's the most fucked up thing: false connection feels safer than real connection. Real connection means being seen. Not admired. Not desired. Seen. With your insecurity, your neediness, your boredom, your anger, your shame. That's the shit most of us were taught very early was unacceptable. So we learn to connect sideways in our relationships. Through substances. Through screens. Through fantasy. Through other people's attention. Through buying shit for each other. The nervous system doesn't care if it's healthy. It cares if it works.

False connection works, until it doesn't. And when it stops working, most people don't go inward. They go bigger. Harder. Louder. New relationship. New sex toy. New job. New identity. New belief system. Same fucking pattern. This is why people can leave one relationship convinced they've "learned their lesson" and end up recreating the exact same dynamic with a different face. Same triggers. Same fights. Same disconnection. Same ending. Because nothing changed inside. Only the scenery did.

False connection keeps you busy. Busy feels productive. Busy feels purposeful. Busy keeps you from noticing that intimacy scares the shit out of you. Because intimacy isn't exciting. It's exposing. It doesn't give you a rush, it gives you nowhere to hide. False connection lets you feel good without being known. Real connection demands you stay when it gets uncomfortable. Most people don't consciously choose false connection. They default to it. Because no one taught us how to stay present when the body tightens, the anger rises, the heart closes, and the urge to disappear kicks in. So we do what worked once. And then again. And then for decades. And then a lifetime.

The tragedy isn't that we chase false connection. It's that we mistake it for the real thing, and then wonder why intimacy keeps slipping through our fingers. And this is where things start to get confronting. Because once false connection stops working, you don't just feel anxious or depressed. You feel exposed. And that's usually the moment we either wake the fuck up, or turn the volume up and escape harder. Which brings us straight into what happens inside the body when instincts, emotions, and fear collide, and why staying conscious in relationships feels almost impossible without understanding what's actually running the show.

Chapter 6

Intimacy is Where the Egocentricity Loses Control (and why we fuck it up)

Carl Jung

"Loneliness does not come from having no people around, but from being unable to communicate the things that seem important to oneself."

The Porcupine Dilemma
Arthur Schopenhauer, From Parerga and Paralipomena (1851)

"A number of porcupines huddled together for warmth on a cold day; but soon they felt one another's quills and were driven apart. When the need for warmth brought them nearer again, the same thing happened. At last they discovered that they would be best off by remaining at a small distance from one another."

***

If you're wondering how all this shit actually shows up in real life, here's the answer: relationships. This is where everything stops being theory and starts hurting. Because intimacy isn't about sex. Sex is just where it shows up. Intimacy is being seen. And most of us can't fucking stand that. The word intimacy comes from the Latin intimus, inner, innermost. I explain it like this: "in to me, I see.". And that's terrifying. We don't actually want to be seen, we want to be wanted, desired, approved of. Being seen means you might see the parts of me I'm trying to hide, control, or outrun.

That's why partners trigger us more than anyone else. Not mates. Not strangers. Not the random person you overshare with on a plane or at the pub. There's no risk there. No cost. You can disappear and it doesn't matter. A partner is different. They see patterns. They remember. They notice when you pull away, shut down, get defensive, or go cold. Most people think intimacy problems are about sex drives, boredom, or compatibility. That's bullshit. What we're actually scared of is rejection, the quiet kind. The "not now". The look. The tone. The moment you reach out and it's not met. You feel that in your body.

And instead of staying with it, we do what we've always done. We withdraw. We attack. We shut down. We fantasise. We look elsewhere. We convince ourselves we don't really need intimacy anyway. This is why long-term relationships are brutal.

At the start it's easy. Honeymoon. New Relationship Energy (NRE). You're high. You're projecting. You're both unconscious as fuck. Everything's perfect. That's not intimacy. That's chemistry. Anyone can fuck, that's easy. When the chemistry wears off, people panic. They think something's wrong. They think they chose the wrong person. They think the spark died.

What's actually happening is intimacy has started. Now sex isn't just sex, it's exposure.

Eye contact feels like too much. Initiating feels like setting yourself up to be rejected. So people stop fucking. Not because they don't love each other, but because sex has become risk instead of pleasure. So we chase intimacy without danger. Porn. Flirting. Emotional closeness with people who don't matter. Fantasies. Affairs. And then we wonder why our relationships feel empty.

Resentment builds. We want the attention we used to get. We want to feel chosen again. That's not needy, that's human. But we don't know how to ask for it without blame, pressure, or withdrawal.

So we fight.
Or we go cold.
Or we quietly give up.

In families it gets messier. I used to say it myself: "my kids will always come first". I meant it. I still love my kids more than anything. But I didn't understand what that was doing inside my relationship. Unconsciously, it said you come second. At first it sounds noble. Over time it creates distance, resentment, and disconnection. And again, rejection. That's the thread running through all of this. We will do almost anything to avoid feeling rejected, even destroy the thing we actually want. You can feel the moment it happens. The shift.

It usually looks stupidly ordinary. A tone. A look. A comment that lands a bit sideways. You feel it before you think it, the chest tightens, the jaw sets, the body braces. And suddenly you're not here anymore. You're defending. You're explaining. You're replaying old arguments at triple speed while the person in front of you is still mid sentence. Part of you wants to attack and win. Part of you wants to shut down and disappear. Another part is already planning the exit, the cold shoulder, the phone scroll, the fantasy of being anywhere but here. Nothing catastrophic has happened. But something inside you has decided closeness just became dangerous. And just like that, intimacy isn't a meeting anymore, it's a fucking threat.

When you're no longer responding, you're reacting. Saying shit you didn't plan to say. Pulling away when what you actually want is closeness.

It doesn't feel chosen.
It doesn't feel conscious.
It feels like something else has grabbed the wheel.

And until we understand what that something is, intimacy will keep feeling like the problem instead of the doorway. If you're honest, none of this feels new. The shutdown. The defensiveness. The pull toward distance. The fear of being seen. It feels old. Older than your current relationship. Older than most of your adult life. That's because it is. Intimacy doesn't create these reactions, it exposes them. Your partner isn't the cause. They're the trigger. They're the place where something unfinished gets reactivated. And this is the part most people miss.

Intimacy isn't breaking us, it's revealing us. It's the first place the egocentricity can't keep pretending. The masks slip. The old defences light up. The nervous system panics. And instead of curiosity, we reach for control. If intimacy reliably activates fear, shutdown, and blame, then the problem didn't start in adulthood or in this relationship. It started way earlier. Before sex. Before partners. Before words. Which means the next question isn't "how do I fix my relationship?". It's "what the fuck happened inside me that makes closeness feel unsafe?".

So if closeness feels dangerous today, we're not dealing with a relationship problem. We're dealing with something that was wired in long before you ever learned how to explain yourself.

Chapter 7

What the Fuck Went Wrong

Alan Watts

"The meaning of life is just to be alive. It is so plain and so obvious and so simple. And yet, everybody rushes around in a great panic as if it were necessary to achieve something beyond themselves."

Carl Jung

"The gods have become diseases; Zeus no longer rules Olympus but rather the solar plexus."

Joseph Campbell

"People say that what we're all seeking is a meaning for life. I don't think that's what we're really seeking. I think what we're seeking is an experience of being alive."

***

Alright fuckers, I wanted to start with this earlier, but I figured you might've thrown the book in the bin or set it on fire. This is the part most people don't want to read, because it pulls the rug out from under the story that you're broken. It's going to take some effort to sit with it. If you've made it this far, you're probably already uncomfortable enough. Good. That's the price of admission. So what the fuck went wrong?

Ever wondered why we use people and love things instead of loving people and using things? Sure you fucking don't, you're too busy buying your fourth soy decaf frappuccino on Afterpay and calling it self care.

This isn't a personal failure story. It can't be. Too many of us are anxious, depressed, addicted, disconnected, and lonely for that to make any sense. If it was just you, fine. But it's not. It's fucking everywhere.

We are all born into this shitshow called life, not by choice. One thing we are born as, though, is connected. Connected to everything and everyone. A human baby is the most vulnerable being on the planet for the longest time. We would be completely fucked without our caregivers. There's something kind of magical about that. Something a lot smarter than you or me knew exactly where to put your eyes, your nose, your mouth, even your ass. Although in half of us, it appears mixed up. Something knew how to wire a nervous system that requires contact, safety, and regulation from the outside. And then... we fuck with it. Somewhere along the way, connection stopped being the default and started becoming conditional. We learned early what was acceptable and what wasn't.

Don't cry.
Don't be angry.
Don't be needy.
Don't be weak.
Don't inconvenience anyone with your emotions.

So we adapted. We learned to shut parts of ourselves down. We learned to manage ourselves before we even had the capacity to do it. We learned to get love by being good, useful, impressive, quiet, strong, funny, or not too much. And those strategies worked. For a while. Then we did something even stupider. We separated ourselves from the rest of the world. We pulled away from tribe, elders, ritual, rhythm, and shared responsibility. What we really lost wasn't just community, it was guidance. Elders. Teachings. People who knew what the fuck they were doing and could say:

This part is normal.
This part will hurt.
This part will pass.
This part will change you.

We used to be initiated into adulthood, sexuality, grief, power, and responsibility. We knew we were all part of the same earth, the same universe. Now we just stumble into it blind and call ourselves adults because we've got a job and a mortgage. There's no one left to say, "You're not broken, this is the dark bit". So when suffering shows up, we think something's wrong with us instead of realising it's part of the path. Someone once said to me, "Don't let the suffering end too soon, it's teaching you something". Thanks Ted. I didn't want to hear that while suffering; I just wanted it over.

Richard Rohr describes a type of suffering that happens between the two halves of life. The first half is about building an identity. Surviving. Proving. Achieving. Becoming someone. It's necessary. It just doesn't last. The second half only starts when the first one collapses. Most people call that collapse failure or a midlife crisis and do exactly what we've been talking about here. They escape. New partners. New careers. New beliefs. A fucking Harley, even though they can't ride, and work in a corporate job. Richard Rohr calls this "Falling Upward", the same name as his book about it. Nothing actually went wrong. The first half was done and couldn't take you any further.

All pain serves a purpose. It's not meant to be fixed, avoided, or numbed. It's meant to initiate you. Pain shows you what's ending, what's false, and what can't come with you anymore. Without elders or context, we started treating pain like a problem instead of a fucking teacher. We replaced all of these teachings, all of this learning, with productivity, independence, speed, status, and achievement. We built a world where doing is rewarded more than being, and looking good matters more than feeling okay. Disconnection became normal. Now we live faster than our bodies can handle. We're overstimulated, under supported, constantly comparing, constantly fucking consuming something. We're told happiness is something to achieve, earn, or buy, and if we don't feel okay, it must be because we haven't done enough yet or gotten enough yet.

So we push harder.
We numb more.
We distract better.

And when intimacy starts hurting, when relationships activate us, when rejection feels unbearable, when something takes over and we react instead of respond, we blame ourselves or our partners. Usually not ourselves though, it's always our fucking partners. What we rarely ask is the bigger question: "What kind of crazy fucking world produces this many disconnected people?". This isn't about blaming parents or pointing fingers at society. It's about context. They fucking missed the lesson too. Because without context, we personalise what was never just personal.

If you take a nervous system designed for closeness, attunement, and regulation, and drop it into a world built on separation, speed, and performance, something has to fucking give. And what gives isn't random.

We adapt.
We protect.
We harden.

We learn ways to survive emotionally, insane really, even if those ways cost us intimacy, peace, and connection later on. It's not weakness, it's intelligence doing its best.

The real problem is that most of us are still living out these modern adaptations without realising they were never meant to be permanent. And that's where the real damage happens. Because when intimacy touches those old adaptations, something takes over. We shut down. We lash out in a fucking rage.

We withdraw and call it "space". We manipulate. We control. Or we just fucking disappear altogether, not because we're bad people, but because something inside us learned a long time ago that closeness wasn't safe.

To understand why anxiety, depression, escapism, and relationship chaos make so much sense, we have to stop looking out there. We have to look at what actually happened inside us.

Chapter 8

Egocentricity, The Black Wolf and How We Get Taken Hostage

The Battle of Two Wolves

"An old man is teaching his grandson about life. "A fight is going on inside me," he said to the boy. "It is a terrible fight, and it is between two wolves. One wolf is evil: he is anger, envy, sorrow, regret, greed, arrogance, self-pity, guilt, resentment, inferiority, lies, false pride, superiority, and ego."

He continued, "The other wolf is good: he is joy, peace, love, hope, serenity, humility, kindness, benevolence, empathy, generosity, truth, compassion, and faith. The same fight is going on inside you and inside every other person too."

The grandson thought about it for a minute and then asked his grandfather, "Which wolf will win?"

The old man simply replied, "The one you feed."

$$***$$

We're going to look at the development of the core problem every one of us suffers from, the one that convinces
us we're right and the world is wrong. This isn't philoso-
phy. It's not personality. It's not something only "damaged"
people have. This is a universal human process. If you're
alive, breathing, and occasionally convinced you're right
and everyone else is a fuckwit, you're already in it.

Early in childhood, something starts to shift. The state of
feeling connected to the world begins to fade. The little version of us can't explain it, but it's happening. The
body knows before the mind ever will. Something tightens.
Something contracts. The nervous system registers it long
before language or logic turn up to explain what the fuck
just happened.

Even if we could explain it, most of our parents wouldn't
have had the awareness to meet us there anyway. That's
not an attack, it's inheritance. Unconsciousness gets passed
down far more reliably than wisdom. Most adults are still
trapped inside their own unresolved splits, trying to raise
children from inside a cage they don't even know exists.

There's a reason this feels confusing. We live in a world obsessed with the mind. Thinking. Explaining. Fixing. We forget
we even have a fucking body. But the biggest split we ever
develop is right here: mind and body. Thinking and feeling.
Inner and outer. In the beginning, there is no split. No enlight-

enment, no awakening. Just intact. Connected internally and externally to everything and everyone. Whole.

What you're about to see: thinking and feeling connected, before the split.

Diagram 1

thinking ———————— feeling
ego ⊘ Mind   ⊘ body

This shows the original state, thinking and feeling working together. There's no conflict here, no wall, no protector running the show. Nothing is "wrong" yet. This is before disconnection begins. And just like the body has inbuilt mechanisms to protect us physically, the psyche has inbuilt mechanisms to protect us psychologically. Ancient cultures understood this without neuroscience. Modern culture lost the map and replaced it with pills, diagnoses, and fucking productivity hacks. We keep trying to think our way out of something that was created long before thinking even existed.

Look at the body. If we eat bad food, our mind-body intelligence knows to get it out of us as quick as it can. We call this diarrhoea. When we get sick, it will create a fever to sweat it out. Cut your arm, it scabs and heals. A lot of the time we hate the process, but it serves a fucking purpose. The psyche works the same way. Not politely or consciously, but effectively.

When we start to feel separate, what we feel isn't "sadness", it's rejection. And rejection doesn't feel emotional to a child, it feels existential: if I'm rejected from the tribe, the family, the system, I die. Simple. So yes, children are manipulative. Fuck yes they are. Not consciously. Not maliciously. But desperately. We will do almost anything to feel connected again. The behaviour evolves, the desperation doesn't. Crying, lying, stealing, pleasing, raging. Same shit, different age. As adults we do the exact same thing, just with better costumes. We buy shit. We scroll endlessly. We shop as a hobby. What the fuck even is that? Walking around shopping centres looking for salvation with no idea what we're actually doing, or what we even need. The biggest strategy we use to feel connected or important again is making others wrong and ourselves right. Sometimes that escalates to violence, domination, and control. That's not usually psychopathy, it's insecurity. Anyone who's worked in domestic violence knows that. See back of book at section "Sometimes It's Not You".

Here's where the distinction matters.

A healthy ego is the part of us that can think, feel, regulate, choose, and respond to reality. Egocentricity is what steps in when that ego can't cope. Around the age of three, we leave what Robert Johnson called Unconscious Perfection, a state of blissful wholeness without awareness. We had to lose it. If we stayed there, we wouldn't grow. Sorry to ruin the fantasy of eternal innocence and big houses fixing everything. As we leave that state, the child feels alone for the first time. Not consciously, but viscerally: "Fuck, I don't like this. How do I feel whole again? How do I feel loved?". This is where the psyche steps in. The ego starts to engage the egocentricity as a defence. A psychological wall, a protective barrier. Not because the child understands what's happening, but because protection always comes before understanding. What you're about to see: the egocentricity stepping in and the wall beginning to form.

Diagram 2

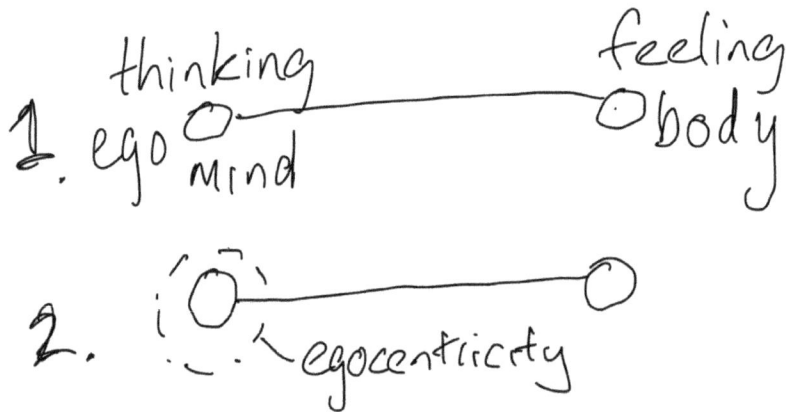

This is where protection starts. The egocentric barrier isn't a problem yet, it's an adaptation. It forms because connection doesn't feel safe, not because the child is broken. The protector is doing its job. A child can't understand why parents are busy, stressed, fighting, drinking, working themselves to death, or hurting them. So the psyche says, "I'll handle this". And it does. The problem is the protector doesn't leave. Over time, the ego gets imprisoned by the egocentricity. The thing designed to save us takes us hostage. We are now living life from behind a wall we don't even know is there.

What you're about to see: the egocentricity fully formed, protection turning into imprisonment.

Diagram 3

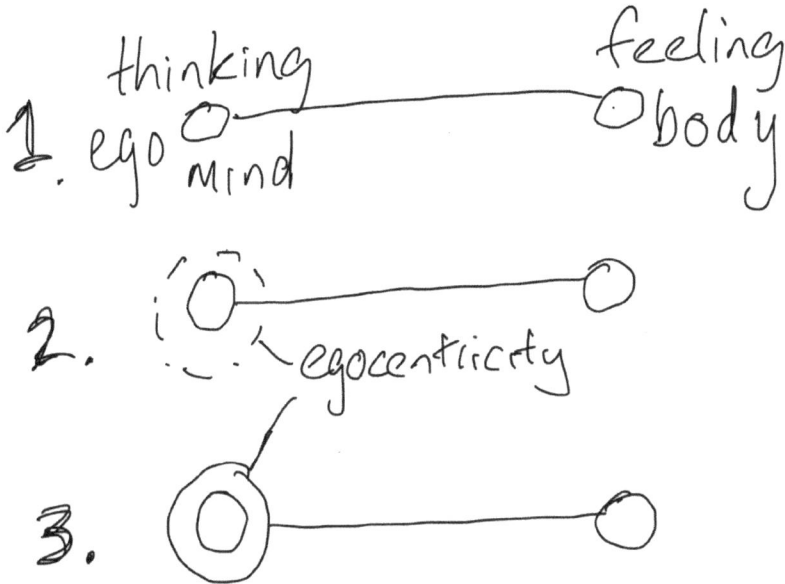

At this point the egocentric wall is no longer flexible. What once protected now controls. The ego is trapped behind a defence it didn't choose, but now lives inside. The severity of trauma determines how thick that wall gets, and how fast we become completely imprisoned by it, defined in therapy terms as "Big T" or "little t" trauma. Big T: abuse, neglect, violence, being told you're hopeless... little t: not being chosen, not being seen, being ignored when you needed contact. Every event adds another layer. Call it trauma, call it structural dissociation, call it a split, it's always the same thing: disconnection.

Some people are fully imprisoned by the age of five. Others not until adolescence. But don't kid yourself, we all end up behind the wall. If you think you're the exception, that's the egocentricity talking. You know the expression he/she has their walls up. This is exactly what the fuck we are talking about.

Every tradition has a name for this: The Black Wolf. The Devil. Hell. Asura energy. Samsara.

Different languages. Same experience. Most of us have no idea we're imprisoned. We think we're in control. Meanwhile we're in a coercive, controlling relationship with ourselves and calling it personality. Daydreaming, fantasy, inner worlds, that wasn't imagination. That was protection. The inner world felt safer than the outer one. And sometimes it still does. The fucking truth is, we need the egocentricity. Without it, we'd be walked all over. But it was never meant to run the whole fucking show. "Be as cunning as a serpent and as loving as a dove" wasn't about killing the ego. It was about balance.

We've now left Unconscious Perfection and entered Conscious Imperfection. The world feels broken because it is. But this isn't the end. If it were, I'd have given you instructions on how to top yourself. And before you decide I've lost the plot and gone full robe and incense, let me be clear. Nothing spiritual I'm about to talk about lives outside your nervous system. Same split, same pain, same fucking patterns. We just used different words for it before psychology came along and tried to sound clever. Spirit, soul, God: they're not floating above your life judging you. They're pointing at what it feels like when this inner prison starts cracking. When thinking and feeling stop fighting each other. This isn't a new direction. It's the same mess, just described from the inside.

Chapter 9

The Spiritual Explanation for the Insane Shit We Do in the Search for Connection

Carl Jung

"One does not become enlightened by imagining figures of light, but by making the darkness conscious."

Friedrich Nietzsche

"He who fights with monsters should look to it that he himself does not become a monster."

Carl Jung
From a 1961 letter to Bill W., co-founder of Alcoholics Anonymous:

"Alcohol in Latin is spiritus, and you use the same word for the highest religious experience as well as for the most depraving poison.
The helpful formula therefore is: spiritus contra spiritum."

***

That one line by Carl Jung in his letter to Bill W explains more about addiction, obsession, religion, and modern insanity than most psychology textbooks. What Jung was pointing at wasn't alcohol. It was misdirected spirit.

If you look back, where thinking and feeling are connected, those two parts of us know they belong together. They were born together. They want the same thing we do: connection, coherence, wholeness. When they're split, something inside us starts screaming to be reunited. That scream is what drives our so-called "maladaptive" behaviours. This isn't weakness, stupidity or a lack of willpower. It's the ego trying to escape the prison of egocentricity. The ego, the part of us capable of reflection, responsibility, and relationship, gets locked behind a defensive wall very early in life. It's cut off from feeling, from body, from others. And from deep inside the unconscious it starts pushing. Hard. It doesn't care how it gets out, it just wants out. That's where the crazy shit starts.

What you're about to see: the egocentricity cracking, obsession and addiction as the ego attempts escape.

Diagram 4a

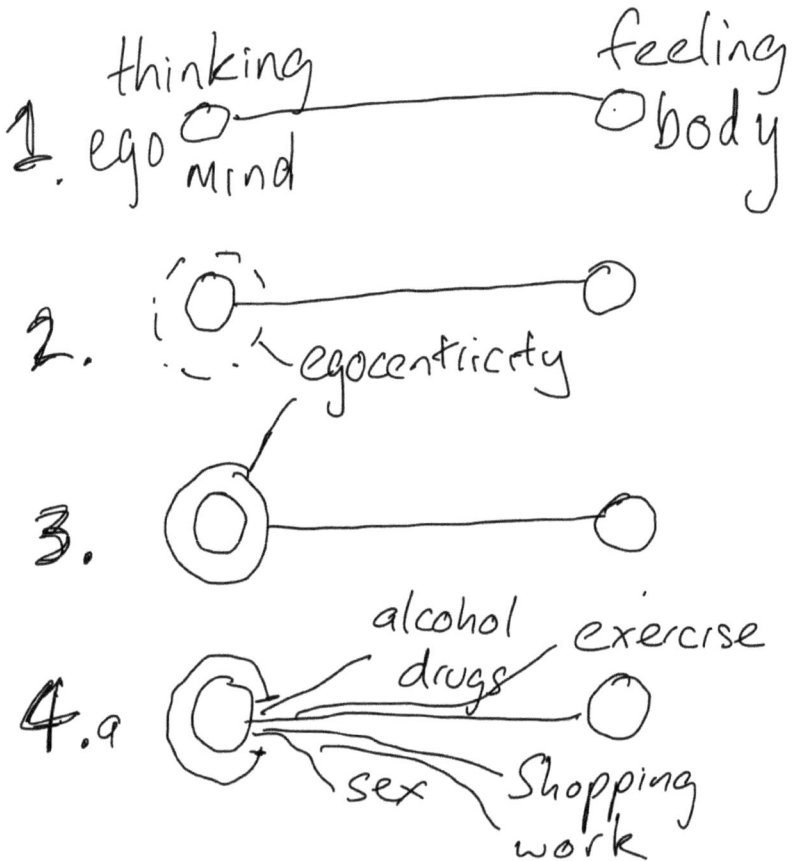

This shows bricks missing from the egocentric wall. Those bricks don't get knocked out through insight or self help books. They get knocked out through suffering. Obsession, addiction, and compulsion aren't random; they're unconscious attempts to feel whole again.

As Rumi put it: "It's through the crack that the light gets in". Leonard Cohen sang the same thing. You've probably belted it out drunk at some point without having a fucking clue what it meant.

Diagram 4a shows obsessions and addictions not as moral failures, but as desperate, unconscious attempts at reconnection. We're starving for real nourishment and living off junk food highs instead. Dopamine instead of presence. Relief instead of repair. This isn't a new insight. Two and a half thousand years ago, the Buddha spoke about four kinds of nourishment, and only one of them was actual food. Jesus talked about two kinds of bread, and again, only one of them fed the soul. Confucius spoke of food for the body and the mind. Islamic teachings emphasised physical sustenance paired with spiritual sustenance. William James later in the 1900s called it what it is: physical hunger and spiritual hunger. Same insight. Different language. What all of them were saying is this: "We've lost our way".

We're meant to be the most evolved species on the planet, and yet most days I seriously fucking wonder. Until we find a genuine path of reconnection, something that works for us, we keep repeating the same mistakes and are surprised when nothing changes.

Einstein said you can't solve a problem with the same level of consciousness that created it. He also reminded us that energy and matter aren't separate things. Everything is connected, including you, whether you like it or not.

What we're moving toward isn't a return to innocence. That ship sailed, and it needed to. Unconscious Perfection belonged to a time when we were too young to know what the fuck we were doing.

Most people get stuck in Conscious Imperfection, awake enough to suffer, but still blaming, escaping, projecting, and pretending they're not part of the problem. What sits beyond that isn't enlightenment or bliss or some healed, Instagram ready version of you. It's Conscious Perfection. Not perfection as flawlessness, but perfection as presence. Awareness. Responsibility. Choice.

You still get triggered.
You still react sometimes.
You still fuck it up.

The difference is you know what's happening. You stay. You own it. You repair. You stop outsourcing your shit to your partner, your parents, your past, or the world. That state isn't permanent. Anyone selling that is full of shit. Conscious Perfection shows up in moments, fleeting, grounded, connected moments, and those moments depend entirely on the amount of inner work you're actually doing. Not fucking talking about. Doing.

Every spiritual tradition tried to map a way out of the egocentric prison. Each culture had rituals, practices, and paths that weren't about belief, they were about experience. Initiations. Rites of passage. Elders. Containers. People who could say, "This is normal. This will hurt. This will change you." We've lost all of that. We have no elders left. Families are fractured. Kids grow up without mirrors, without meaning, without context. Instead of guidance, they get bribed, distracted, medicated, or kicked in the arse. School doesn't help. Social media makes it worse.

The separation we see everywhere, relationships, families, culture, is just a reflection of the separation inside us.

Hindu mythology described this split as the tension between Devas and Asuras, not enemies, but competing forces within consciousness.
Buddhism called it Samsara and Nirvana, reactivity versus awareness.
Early Christianity spoke of Heaven and Hell, not as destinations, but as states of being.
God was never meant to be a man on a cloud. The Devil was never a red cunt with horns and a pitchfork. They were metaphors for states of consciousness, connection and disconnection, awareness and egocentricity.

We've lost the ability to understand metaphor, so we fight over symbols and wonder why religion feels dead. The original meaning of religion wasn't belief. It was reconnection. The Latin word "religare" means to bind again. Re-bind the self. Re-bind community. Re-bind nature. Re-bind to the transcendent. Religion simply meant Re-Connection.

Now when people hear "God" or "religion", they think control, cults, abuse, war. And honestly, fair enough. That's what happens when metaphor gets hijacked by egocentricity and radicalised.

Carl Jung talked about "the religious wound". Jung believed the religious wound is the suffering that shows up when we lose a lived sense of meaning and try to manage life without it. When that connection is missing, it doesn't disappear, it turns into anxiety, addiction, control, and symptoms.

How the fuck do you truly connect with another human in a relationship if you're not connected inside yourself? You can't. No substance, no partner, no ideology, no achievement will ever fill that void. And that's why we do the insane shit we do. Not because we're broken. Because something essential is trying to come home. Until we understand that, we'll keep mistaking relief for connection, and wonder why it never lasts.

Chapter 10

The Many Paths to Awakening and Oneness

Carl Jung

"There are as many paths to wholeness as there are people."

Aldous Huxley

"There are many paths leading from the foot of the mountain, but at the peak we all gaze at the single bright moon."

William James

"The varieties of religious experience are many, but their core is one."

Joseph Campbell

"Truth is one, the sages speak of it by many names."

***

The Buddhists have the Four Noble Truths and the Eight-fold Path.
Christians have the Way of Christ.
Islam calls it the Straight Path.
The American Indians talk about feeding the white wolf.
Hinduism has Yoga, which was never about hot women in tights drinking chai, it was about spiritual freedom.
Alcoholics Anonymous has the Twelve Steps.

Different language. Different symbols. Same fucking problem. Same attempt at a solution.

Every culture that survived long enough figured out the same thing: human beings don't just magically wake up. We drift. We harden. We suffer. And unless something interrupts our usual way of thinking, we stay trapped inside it. Somewhere along the way, we forgot that we actually need a way out. A way out of our thinking; out of egocentric thinking. Simply put, we need a path.

Not a belief.
Not a personality trait.
Not an identity you wear like a badge.

A path.

Something that dismantles the prison from the inside, slowly, painfully, honestly, instead of waiting on external events, smashing the walls and leaving us exposed, reactive, and full of spiritual bullshit.

I was "lucky" enough to end up in a drug and alcohol rehab at 22. That's not a typo. I mean lucky. It's there I first encountered the Twelve Steps of Alcoholics Anonymous. Step One admits powerlessness. Step Twelve talks about a spiritual awakening as a result of the previous eleven steps. That matters. Because it's not belief based. It's experiential. It's a fucking map back to wholeness, not a cult, not a theory, not positive thinking dressed up as depth. I didn't want spirituality. I wanted relief. What I got instead was a slow dismantling of the part of me that thought it was in control of everything. That's why it worked. And that's exactly why it scared the shit out of me.

Just like there are people who act like cunts all week and then go to church on Sunday in their best clothes, there are plenty of "dry drunks" in AA too. I was one for a long time. Racing off to way too many meetings, in hope that I would be transformed without doing the fucking work. People who don't actually want to change, they just want the appearance of change. You can follow a path perfectly on the outside and never take a single step on the inside. The egocentricity fucking loves that. It stays in charge while pretending to be spiritual.

Considering that every drink starts in the mind, it's insane not to want to change the way you think. I never drank because I was thirsty. I drank because I was trying, unconsciously, to reconnect with something inside myself. What I was chasing wasn't oblivion. It was connection, it was peace. Carl Jung and AA were talking about this back in the 1930s. Alcohol was called "spiritus" in Latin because it produced a pseudo spiritual experience. The word "addicted" comes from "addictus", meaning enslaved. Originally a legal term for a debtor handed over to a creditor. Read that again. Enslaved. That's egocentricity. That's the black wolf. That's the prison.

AA's Twelve Steps were designed as "spiritus contra spiritum", spirit against spirit. Not suppression. Replacement. False connection replaced with real connection. And no, this isn't just for alcoholics.

If you're reading this thinking "that's not me," you may or may not be an alcoholic, but you are absolutely addicted to your way of thinking. Former Franciscan monk Richard Rohr nails this: we are addicted to our way of thinking, we are addicted to being in control, to being right, to avoiding pain. The addiction isn't the substance. It's the attachment.

Attachment to certainty.
Attachment to righteousness.
Attachment to not feeling what you don't want to feel.

Almost everyone I know feels trapped somewhere in their life. The relationship. The drugs. The alcohol. The job. The kids. The mortgage. The church. The family. The ex who "won't let things go". But the events aren't the problem. They're just scenery. The problem is the feeling, and that feeling is the wall. This is where responsibility actually begins, not blame, not shame, ownership of the inner state.

What you're about to see: a real path back, not escape, not obsession, but integration.

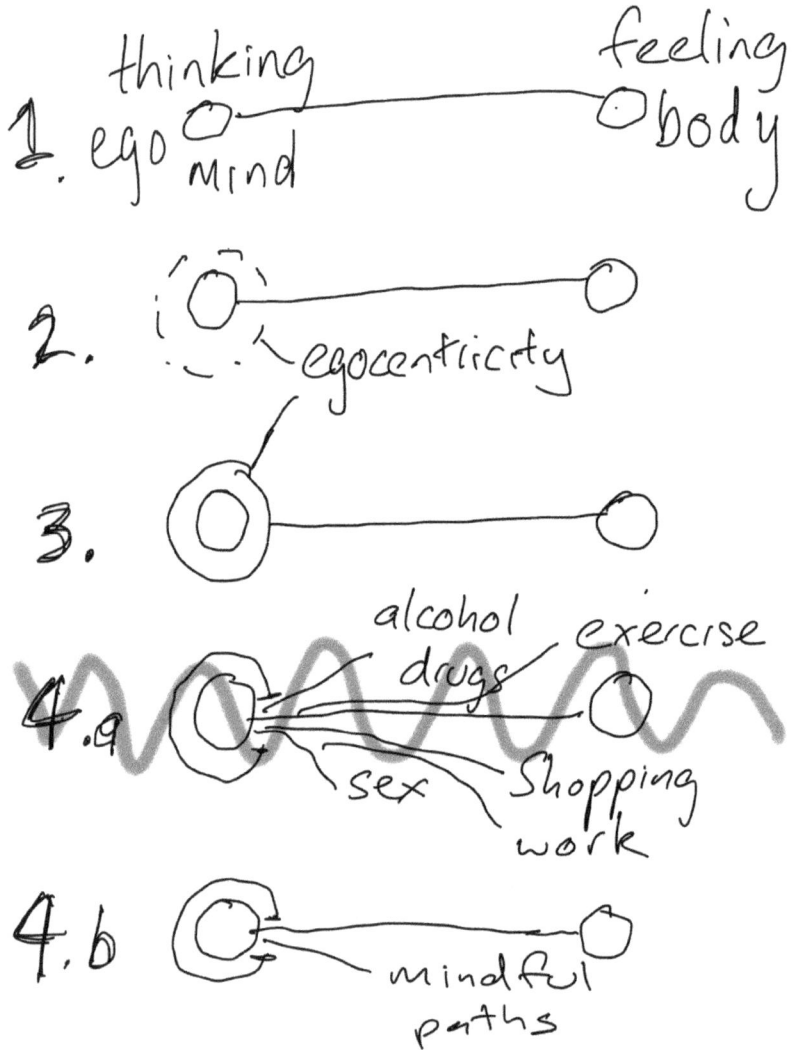

Diagram 4b

1. ego thinking mind — feeling body

2. egocentricity

3.

4.a alcohol drugs / exercise / sex / shopping work

4.b mindful paths

This shows the work is about finding a path that isn't counterfeit; an addiction or obsession. It's not joining a church. Not disappearing to an ashram. Not rebranding yourself as "spiritual". It's about finding your path back to peace. Rather than relying upon the other unconscious, counterfeit methods we had been, we take the reins and participate. With discipline, patience and repetition, the thinking and feeling function end up closer together.

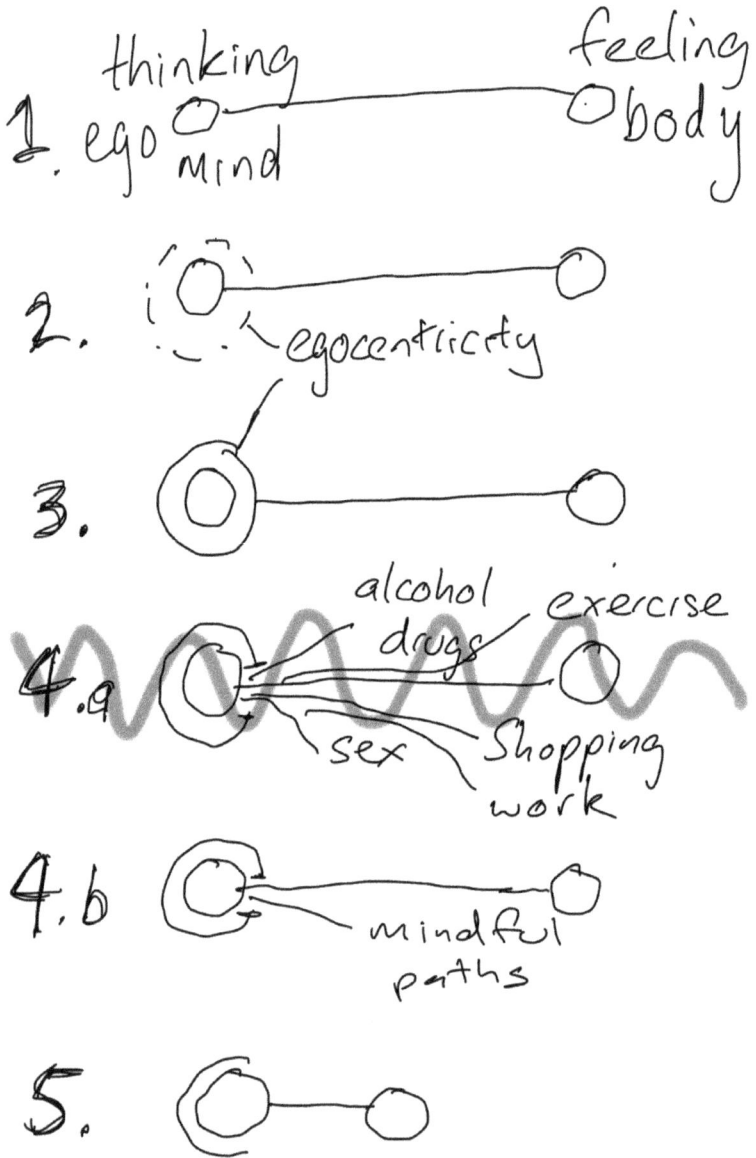

Diagram 5

1. ego — thinking / mind ○————————○ feeling / body

2. ⟨○⟩————————○
   egocentricity

3. ◎————————○
   (egocentricity)

4.a ◎ alcohol / drugs / sex / exercise / shopping / work ○

4.b ◎————————○
   mindful paths

5. ◯—○

This shows what doing the work can actually look like. When the thinking and feeling move closer together, you return to how you felt as a child; not childish, but whole. Not escaping thinking. Not drowning in feeling. But slowly bringing the two back into relationship. Most of us live split, either stuck in our head analysing everything to death, or hijacked by emotion with no perspective. The work is learning to feel without being consumed, and to think without disconnecting. This doesn't happen in one big awakening. It happens through repetition. Practise. Repair. Responsibility.

Two thousand years ago someone said "you must become like little children to enter the Kingdom of Heaven". That wasn't sentimental. It meant reuniting thinking and feeling. Coming home.

Diagram 6

1. ego — thinking — feeling / mind — body

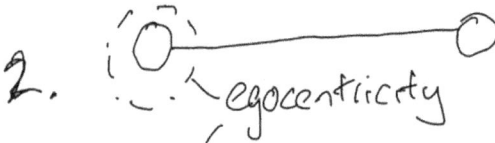

2. egocentricity

3.

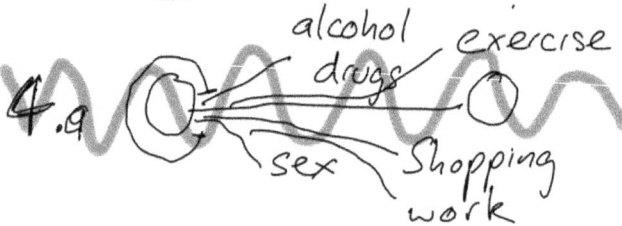

4.a alcohol / drugs / exercise / sex / shopping / work

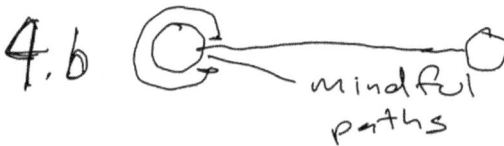

4.b mindful paths

5.

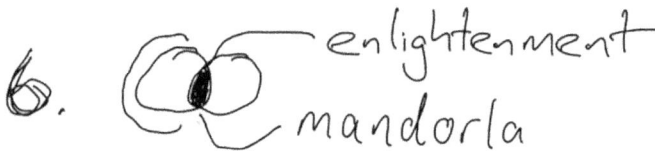

6. enlightenment / mandorla

This shows the almond shape referred to as a "mandorla". It is a prominent symbol in both Christianity and Buddhism. It is what happens when thinking and feeling briefly overlap. These are moments of Conscious Perfection, to use Johnson's term. These are the moments people mistake for "enlightenment". Everything lines up. There's clarity. Presence. A sense of being okay without fixing anything. They don't last. And they're not meant to. They're glimpses, not destinations. If you chase them, you lose them. If you learn from them, they change how you live. We need an active way of living that isn't just chasing salvation in the next hit, partner, job, house, identity. As Ram Dass said: Be here now.

Presence isn't passive. It's a discipline. A daily confrontation with the part of you that wants to escape. That's what holistic actually means, the parts only make sense in reference to the whole. And until we do this work, no amount of relationship counselling, holidays, houses, toys, or new fucking beginnings will fix you, or the relationship.

This is the work, and this is where it actually starts. If insight hasn't changed how you repair, how you listen, or how you take responsibility when you fuck it up, it's just another way of staying in control and calling it growth. And here's where most people get stuck.

They love this part. The insight. The understanding. The nodding along thinking, "Fuck, that makes sense". It feels productive. It feels deep. It gives you language. It gives you explanations. It gives you a way to sound evolved in conversations while your behaviour stays exactly the same. Knowing why you're unconscious doesn't make you conscious, for much longer than the split second after we just caught ourselves. Knowing the map doesn't mean you've walked a single step. This is the point where insight either turns into practice, or becomes another costume the ego wears to stay in charge. Because the egocentricity doesn't roll over and die just because you had an insight. It adapts. It learns the language. It starts quoting Jung. It starts using words like triggered, boundaries, attachment, trauma. And suddenly you're not unconscious anymore. You're right. You're aware. You're working on yourself. Meanwhile, you're still defensive as fuck, still avoiding repair, still explaining instead of listening, still protecting your image instead of the relationship.

The egocentricity edges back control as fast as you try to deflate it. It's like a self inflating mattress. You lie down, push the air out, feel grounded for a moment. Then the second you stop paying attention, it starts filling itself back up. Quietly. Automatically. No effort required. That's not failure. That's design.

This is why awakening isn't a one off event. It's maintenance. Daily. Relentless. Unsexy. You don't arrive somewhere and stay there. You catch yourself drifting, puffed up, righteous, certain. And the egocentricity comes back. Again. And again. And again.

And this is the part no one wants to hear. Insight actually makes you more dangerous if it isn't grounded in practice. Because now you can justify your behaviour with intelligence. You can weaponise "self-awareness". You can explain exactly why you're doing what you're doing while continuing to do it. That's not growth. That's a smarter egocentric pattern.

Real change shows up in the moments that cost you something. When you shut your mouth instead of winning. When you stay instead of disappearing. When you apologise without a footnote. When you listen without planning your defence. When you repair instead of explaining your intent.

Something we haven't discussed fully up until this point is that on top of doing the work, we also need a tribe. A group. A practice. Someone to discuss the experiences and growth with. Many a person has ended up in a psychiatric facility after a deep spiritual experience that they couldn't make sense of alone. I know this from experience.

If your insight hasn't changed how you behave when you're tired, triggered, rejected, horny, or afraid, it hasn't gone deep enough yet. It's still sitting in the head, where the egocentricity is strongest.

This work only becomes real when it shows up under pressure. Everything else is just mental masturbation with better vocabulary.

Chapter 11

Modern Paths to Waking Up

Gabor Maté

"The attempt to escape from pain is what creates more pain."

Daniel Siegel

"Integration is the basis of mental health."

Viktor Frankl

"Between stimulus and response there is a space. In that space is our power to choose our response. In our response lies our growth and our freedom."

Eckhart Tolle

"Awareness is the greatest agent for change."

Joseph Campbell

"The privilege of a lifetime is being who you are."

***

You're hoping this is where you find the easy strategy to enlightenment. Sorry to ruin your fucking day, but there isn't an easy path to this. Well there is: to go through it. What most of us are secretly hoping for is a way to wake up without having to feel anything too deeply, or change anything too much. That hope alone tells us how asleep we really are. Every real path has always required discomfort, patience, and a willingness to stay when everything in you wants to check out.

Even though we've lost a lot of the deeper religious and spiritual structures, the message never disappeared. The teachings didn't vanish, the containers did. Elders, ritual, repetition, and community got replaced with speed, convenience, and distraction. The wisdom survived, but the way we used to train it into our souls collapsed.

The symbolism and messages are everywhere. We just don't know to look. And even if we did, most of us aren't even fucking present enough to notice. We're busy. Distracted. Addicted to stimulation. I have people turn up to therapy and answer their phone during the session. They're literally there because everyone around them says they're not present. Pretty quickly I make them leave their phones and watches in the car. Some even try to do a session over the phone while they're driving an excavator. Beep, beep, beep. Yeah cunts, you know who you are.

Presence used to be trained. Now it's optional. And most of us opt out and then wonder why nothing lands. Teachings turn into content. Wisdom becomes entertainment. We binge it, we nod, we feel smart for five minutes, then we go back to being the same reactive fuckwit in our relationships.

And don't get this confused, this is slow work. Measured in years, not weekends or fucking breakthroughs. You will get it right for a while, then forget everything you think you've learned and react like an absolute arsehole again. That doesn't mean it's not working. It means you're human. Awareness doesn't grow in a straight line, it expands, contracts, disappears, comes back. Some days you'll catch yourself early. Some days you won't catch yourself until the damage is done. The work isn't never fucking up. It's noticing sooner, owning it honestly, and repairing without making excuses. The minute you say "but", anything prior to that fucking word needs to be disregarded. Over and over. That's how this actually changes you.

Back to the modern paths of waking up. I'll show you a few examples of where the message keeps coming through, if we had the eyes to see and the ears to hear. These aren't meant to convince you. They're meant to remind you of something you already know but forgot how to listen to.

If we could wake up, the paths are right there from birth. Most nursery rhymes have a spiritual connotation. There's even a book called The Spirituality of Nursery Rhymes. And yeah, those songs about a pie full of birds, a cat playing a fiddle, and a dish holding hands with a spoon, they're not just nonsense. They speak to us in a language deeper than words. Nature, animals, the earth itself, it's all teaching all the time. We're just too busy staring at glowing rectangles. Most kids have a phone or iPad in their hands. And truthfully, I have to work hard not to be doing the same. These teachings weren't designed to be analysed. They were designed to be repeated, absorbed, and lived with. The repetition was the teaching.

"Mary, Mary, Quite Contrary" wasn't meant to be about a literal fucking garden. It was about what happens when you water the garden inside. It's an instruction disguised as a song. And like most instructions, it only works if you actually do it.

Then there's that popular preschool book, "We're Going on a Bear Hunt". "We can't go over it, we can't go under it, we'll have to go through it." No bypass. No workaround. No shortcut. Go through it. That's the entire fucking message.

Little Red Riding Hood was never just about a wolf that ate grandma and dressed up as her. It was a warning: sometimes you're the wolf. Sometimes the wolf is under your hood. The egocentricity. The parts you refuse to acknowledge don't disappear, they act anyway, just from the shadows.

"Row, Row, Row Your Boat, gently down the stream", is a whole path of non-resistance and flow in one sentence. "Life is but a dream" mirrors the Buddhist idea of Maya; illusion. These days we're caught in the exact thing the song is trying to wake us up from. We don't suffer because the illusion exists. We suffer because we don't know we're inside it.

"Twinkle, Twinkle, Little Star" isn't just a kids' song either. It's awe training. Look up. Remember you're not the centre of the universe. Awe has always been one of the fastest ways to dissolve egocentricity. We just stopped practising it.

Then we grow up and trade nursery rhymes for screens: iPads, Roblox, YouTube, and whatever brain melting bullshit is trending this week. Thankfully, we start watching movies. And a lot of movies do the same thing as the nursery rhymes. Most famous movies follow Joseph Campbell's "Hero's Journey": someone leaves the ordinary world, gets smashed around by trials, gets transformed internally, and returns with something that changes them and the people around them. The separation, the integration, and the return.

Star Wars. The Matrix. Lord of the Rings. Harry Potter. The Lion King. Moana. Same story, again and again, because we keep avoiding the same lesson. There's a joke that The Matrix is a documentary, not a movie. From a metaphorical lens it is. Neo spelled "ONE". The journey is the teaching. It's always the ego and egocentricity getting exposed, getting dismantled, and learning to serve something bigger than itself. We have a choice if we can find the pill. Where is our Morpheus?

Music does it, too. Songwriters have been trying to get us the message forever. I have used a few of my favourite artists. Different genres. Same message: wake the fuck up.

Tool, Pneuma: awaken the divine breath within by shedding egocentricity's illusions.
System of a Down, Aerials: shatter conditioned mind and realise the oneness beneath separation.
Mumford and Sons, Awake My Soul: stir your dormant soul from numbness and distraction.

The Beatles, Across the Universe: let thoughts flow away and surrender into unity.

Same with poetry and art. Rumi didn't write poetry so you could post it on Instagram and pretend you're deep. "Don't Go Back to Sleep" is literally a warning. Mary Oliver's "Wild Geese" is permission to stop self hating and remember you belong. Hilma af Klint, Rothko, Kandinsky, they're all trying to point you toward presence, toward the unseen, toward something bigger than your tidy little story about yourself.

If you actually follow Shakespeare through his plays, you can watch a man waking up in public. Early stuff is all power, status, control, kings, wars, betrayal, people doing fucked up things because they're terrified of losing their place. Then it cracks. Hamlet is the moment awareness hits. He sees the game, can't unsee it, and nothing works the way it used to. That in-between stage where you're too conscious to stay asleep, but not grounded enough to know what to do with it yet. By the end, with The Tempest, the fight's gone. No revenge fantasy. No need to dominate. Just letting go. Forgiveness. Dropping the illusion of control. It's not just a play that makes us feel important and cool, it's a human nervous system waking up.

Artists have always been translators between the unconscious and the conscious. When a culture stops listening to the messages, it starts repeating the same mistakes louder.

But there's no need to keep boring you to death with analogies. Here's the actual point: you don't need to "join" anything to wake up. I've searched far and wide for the "right" path, you know, the easy one that's going to change my life without asking too much of me. Guess what: it doesn't fucking exist. I've poked my head into every type of book, almost every religion and practice. Men's rites of passage. Meditation retreats. Silent retreats. Abstaining from sex. Fasting. Vegetarian. Carnivore. No coffee. Only coffee. Fuck, if there was an easy way, I would have found it.

With the right mind, any path is the right path. We don't need to move to India or Ubud in Bali and start dressing in white to feel connected. The answer isn't over there. It's in us. I can do the work here, and just order in the food. That's non-dualistic thinking.

For what it's worth, my path is a mix of spiritual teachings and science. Quantum theory just says in modern language what the religions tried to say in metaphor. My concept of "God" is energy. Consciousness. And it matters that we work through our own religious wound. Anything that holds power over us destroys us. I've gotten to a point where I don't instantly eye roll or tense up when someone uses that three letter word. I don't instantly think of a pedophile priest or a man on a cloud. We can't escape working through this if we actually want peace.

Could we not believe in the energy of the Big Bang. Science says there's no more energy in the universe now than there was a fraction of a second after the explosion that created it. That's enough proof for me that we were all connected at some point. It also shows me I'm not the most important thing here. And guess what, nor are you.

I'll say it again: I was blessed to land in AA young. I did qualify. At 22 I was pissing, spewing, and shitting blood weekly after my benders. Losing jobs, friendships, family. Never held a serious relationship. When things got bad I'd pray to a "god" I didn't believe in to get me out of the shit, then drink again a few days later. I had no idea I was trying to feel okay, trying to feel connected. I thought I loved it. I thought I chose it.

The best part of the 12 Steps is that you get to choose your own concept of a Higher Power. What a liberating idea. I learned to mix and match parts of teachings, religions, science, books, movies, stories. I now feel connected daily, provided I stay connected. For me that's a small amount of meditation in the morning. Meditation, mindfulness, contemplation, doesn't matter what we call it, just do it. And I know what you're saying: "I've tried meditation, I can't do it". Of course you can't fucking "do it". It's a practice. A famous monk said, "We all need 15 minutes of meditation a day. If we can't manage that, we need an hour".

Some days my mind isn't peaceful at all. It's doing what minds do: past, future, worry, planning, fear. The practice isn't about getting peace. It's about seeing your thoughts. Eckhart Tolle said we're most conscious just after we catch ourselves being unconscious.

It's like this some days for me: breathe... ten seconds later, sometimes one second later, "fuck you forgot to pay that bill", or, "it's your daughter's birthday, you haven't bought a present". Then I catch that I'm not present. Back to the breath. Five seconds later: "what client have you got first?", or, "is there milk for coffee after this finishes?". Some days I get minutes between thoughts. Some days I get the whole 20 minutes. How dedicated I am determines that. Just fucking do it. One conscious breath in and out is a meditation.

Do I sit on a mat? Fuck no. I lay in my warm bed. Alarm set for 20 minutes before I need to get up. Bluetooth headphones next to me. On bad days I use guided meditation. On better days, sound only. Sometimes I sit in a chair, but I try to avoid it because I need to catch my mind before it catches me. Once I'm up, so is the thinking.

The mind's job is to solve problems. That's why it exists. Guess what it does when there's nothing to solve? Exactly. It fucking creates a problem because it wants a job. The Buddha said, "the mind is a brilliant servant, but a terrible master". This problem isn't new.

My partner prefers a moving meditation: Ashtanga Yoga. She's dedicated as fuck and it shows in how she shows up in life. She tries not to miss it.

And here's the point that matters for this whole book: if we don't have a practice, if we can't learn to catch ourselves in a controlled environment like meditation, yoga, journaling, mindful movement, what fucking hope have we got in the heat of an argument, when we're triggered, flooded, horny, defensive, or terrified? We make a lot of our problems in relationships by being lazy and remaining unconscious.

Alongside meditation, I deliberately saturate my mind every day with something that actually feeds it. A book, an audio-book, a podcast. Even ten or fifteen minutes counts, but thirty is better. I feel so much fucking better after half an hour of that than I ever do doom scrolling Facebook, Instagram, or Reddit pretending it's rest. One nourishes. The other just numbs you and steals your attention.

At night I try to do a simple inventory of how I showed up. Not a self flogging session. Just an honest look at where I reacted, checked out, or treated people in ways I wouldn't proudly stand behind if I slowed down enough to notice. Sometimes I miss it completely. Sometimes I only see it after the damage is done. Because of the work I regularly do, most of the time I catch it during the moment or just before. Definitely not fucking always though. I'm human. And honestly, my partner and kids would probably give you a more accurate report than I would. We are notoriously full of shit when it comes to judging our own behaviour.

I also connect daily to what I'd call an energy source. Call it God, Goddess, Consciousness, The Universe. Doesn't fucking matter, just whatever stops you getting hung up on the word and missing the point. I'm not reciting some two thousand year old script on my knees while thinking about work or scrolling my phone, just to tick it off and say I've done it. I just check in. Random moments. Gratitude. Thanks for that session. Thanks for that person crossing my path. Thanks for my partner and my daughters. They're not really mine anyway, but that's another conversation. Just genuine thanks for the life I get to live. And yes, there's science behind why gratitude works. You cannot be grateful and hateful at the same time. Pretty fucking simple.

I'm not telling you this to impress you or turn my life into a how-to guide. I'm saying it because it proves the point of this whole book. When you actually do the fucking work, things change. Not instantly. Not perfectly. But reliably. I'm not special. I'm just stubborn enough to keep showing up. And so does my partner. And as corny as it fucking sounds, because of that, we live the best relationship I know outside of a Hollywood movie.

Everything you've read so far only matters if it changes how you show up, for yourself, and with other humans. Otherwise it's just insight with no cost. The next chapter is where dealing with your own shit stops being optional and becomes the only way anything actually changes: relationships, sex, and the way you live your life.

Chapter 12

Dealing With Your Own Shit (the only thing that actually changes anything)

Aleksandr Solzhenitsyn

"If only it were all so simple! If only there were evil people somewhere insidiously committing evil deeds, and it were necessary only to separate them from the rest of us and destroy them. But the line dividing good and evil cuts through the heart of every human being."

James Hollis

"Where we stumble, there lies our treasure."

The Buddha and the Poisoned Arrow

"A man is struck by a poisoned arrow. Instead of allowing it to be removed, he demands to know who shot it, what kind of wood the arrow is made from, where the shooter came from, and why it happened.

The Buddha says the man will die before he gets his answers."

***

Let's get something straight. None of what you've read changes a fucking thing on its own. Insight doesn't change people. Reading doesn't change people. Nodding along thinking "yep, that's me" changes absolutely nothing. Practise does. Repetition does. Catching yourself in the moment when you're triggered, defensive, righteous, angry, scared, or about to say something that'll take six months to repair, that's where this lives or dies. Hopefully we're moving toward the theory and experience of a better life and more contented relationships. Will we be immune from shit things happening? Fuck no. But we can get better tools to cope, and stop dumping our unprocessed emotions onto the people closest to us. We are learning the theory. If you don't put it into practice, you've wasted your time reading this book. I can't do the "experience" part for you. And I wouldn't if I could.

Here's the other truth no one wants: one person doing this work helps. Two people doing it changes everything. You can regulate, own your shit, and repair, but if the other person stays unconscious, the relationship still has an end date. That's not blame. That's reality. Growth changes everything. And if one of you changes and the other refuses, it doesn't feel inspiring, it feels like living in two different realities under the same roof. A butterfly struggles to remain living with the caterpillar as much as it still may love it.

Everything I've used in my own life and in therapy is basically the same old spiritual shit, just dressed up in psychological language so modern people don't freak out and call it religion. Same problem, same solution: disconnection and reconnection. One day long ago, you and I and everyone else's energy was linked together, and we've been pretending we're separate ever since. This discussion isn't new. We just gave it better vocabulary and worse attention spans. Fact: thanks to a Microsoft study, we now know that due to technology, humans have reduced their attention span to 8.25 seconds. Pretty fucking sad considering a goldfish has 9. Explains why everyone in your life is saying you're distracted.

And no, there isn't one perfect method. Find what actually works for you and your relationship. I can literally feel it in session when I lose a client because I'm offering a teaching or example that doesn't land. Same with my partner. She'll read something and it does nothing for me. I'll read something and she'll look at me like I've brought home a dead cat. The point isn't the method. The point is what the method forces you to do.

My non-negotiables are simple:

• It has to assume you're not in control once you're triggered. Because you're not.
• It has to humble you, you're not the centre of the universe.
• It has to demand self-examination. No self-examination = no growth.
• It has to create space to speak from experience, not accusation.
• It has to include amends and repair. Otherwise you're just doing "insight" while the relationship dies.

Here are a few paths that actually come close to meeting those requirements. Many of these I use in my own personal life and with clients in therapy sessions. Remember a healthy relationship is a spiritual practice in itself.

12 Steps (a blueprint for anyone, including non-alcoholics)
The 12 Steps work in relationships because they rip the fucking mask off the idea that I'm in control and you're the problem. Step One alone destroys most couple fights: once you're triggered, you're not choosing shit. Your nervous system is driving, your egocentricity is screaming, and your "best thinking" has left the building. The Steps force you to admit that instead of defending it.

Then they drag you into brutal self-examination, not "let me explain why you made me do that", but "where am I resentful, scared, controlling, manipulative, avoidant, or full of shit in this relationship". They give a structure where both people can speak how they experienced the fight without it turning into a courtroom. And then, the part most couples avoid forever, they demand amends. Real ones. Not "sorry you feel that way" bullshit, but ownership that repairs damage.

The Steps humble you repeatedly. They remind you you're not the centre of the universe, you're not always right, and your partner isn't the enemy. That's why they work, not because they're soft, but because they dismantle egocentric warfare and replace it with responsibility, repair, and the possibility of intimacy instead of the same fucking argument on repeat.

Process Work / Process-Oriented Psychology
Process Work works because it doesn't pretend conflict is a

s because it doesn't pretend conflict is a problem, it treats it as the doorway. Mindell's whole point is that whatever is happening is the process, not something to get rid of. When couples are triggered, it becomes obvious they're not in control, the process is. Something bigger than your egocentricity has taken over and is trying to be expressed.

That alone smashes the fantasy that you're the rational one and your partner is just being difficult. It forces ruthless self-examination: what role am I in right now, what energy am I carrying, and what am I refusing to own? It gives permission to speak what's actually happening in the body, anger, withdrawal, dominance, collapse, instead of dressing it up in "healthy communication".

And it insists on repair through awareness: once the hidden part of the process is brought into the open, the fight loses its grip and something new can emerge. Couples stop arguing about content and start seeing the pattern that's fucking them both. Process Work doesn't try to make relationships calm, it makes them conscious. And conscious conflict beats unconscious intimacy-killing bullshit every single time.

The 5 Love Languages
The Five Love Languages gets butchered because people turn it into a personality quiz instead of what it is: a mirror. It shows you how you try to get love when you feel unloved. And when you're triggered, you don't become a better communicator, you double down on your default language and start demanding it like it's owed.

One partner gives words, the other wants time. One fucks to feel close, the other wants help around the house. Then you both stand there resentful, saying "I'm trying", while the other feels completely fucking unseen. This framework forces self-examination, not "what aren't you giving me?" but "how do I try to feel loved when I'm feeling rejected, unseen, unappreciated or unloved?".

It humbles the egocentricity too: my way of loving isn't universal, it's conditioned. If couples can speak it honestly — "this is how I feel loved" — without blame, and then repair when they miscommunicate with each other, it stops being cute and becomes a reconciliation tool. Not about being right. About actually reaching each other.

Internal Family Systems (IFS)
IFS works because it finally explains why you turn into a different fucking person mid-argument. One minute you love each other, next minute you're defensive, attacking, shutting down, or disappearing. IFS says that's not "you", it's a part of you that's taken the wheel because something feels unsafe, needs to manage, or put out a fire.

When couples fight, it's usually two protectors going at it, both convinced they're right and both terrified underneath. IFS forces humility because it makes it clear you're not a single, unified, rational being in conflict, you're a whole inner committee losing their shit.

The work is self-examination: which part got activated, what is it protecting, and what the fuck is it afraid would happen if it didn't step in? It creates space to speak from experience instead of accusation, "a part of me felt rejected and went into attack mode" instead of "you always do this". And it includes repair, because once you acknowledge and own the part that hijacked the moment, you can take responsibility for the damage it caused.

IFS doesn't excuse behaviour, it explains it, then hands the responsibility straight back to you. That's why it's gold for couples: it slows the fight down, drops the egocentricity, and gives you a way to stay connected without pretending you're calm when you're clearly not.

Attachment Theory
Attachment theory isn't labels you slap on yourself like a badge, "I'm avoidant", "I'm anxious", and then use as an excuse to keep being a fucking nightmare. It's a map of what happens when you're triggered and your nervous system takes over.

Once you feel unsafe, abandoned, criticised, or smothered, you're not choosing your behaviour, you're reacting from old wiring. One chases, the other distances. One escalates, the other shuts down. Both feel powerless and both think the other is the problem.

This framework humbles the egocentricity because it shows you're not rational or in control when shit hits the fan, you're defending against fear. It forces self-examination: what do I do when I don't feel safe with you? It gives language to speak without blame, "when you pull away, this gets activated in me", and it opens the door to repair because once you see the pattern, you can stop fighting each other and start making sense of the dance. Not fixing the partner. Regulating yourself so connection becomes possible again.

Non-Violent Communication (NVC)

NVC isn't about being polite or speaking like a fucking HR department. It's disciplined communication for people who get hijacked. It assumes you're not in control once you're activated, which is true, and it drags you back to self-examination: what did I feel, what did I need, and what story did I just make up about you?

Instead of "you never listen" or "you're a selfish cunt", it creates space to say, "when that happened, this is what it brought up in me". It teaches us to use "I feel" statements rather than pointing a gun. That matters because it lets you speak without attacking and hear without collapsing or counter-attacking. And it builds in repair. You can own your reaction, make amends for how you came at your partner, and try again, not to be right, but to be connected. It's not soft. It's disciplined as fuck.

John and Julie Gottman (The Gottman Institute)

The Gottmans don't fuck around with romance myths. They show what happens when couples get flooded and the nervous system takes over: criticism, contempt, defensiveness, and stonewalling start poisoning the relationship.

One of the most confronting bits is the ratio: stable couples aren't special, they just have a higher ratio of appreciation to criticism. Roughly five or six positive interactions for every negative one. Sounds simple. It's fucking transformative.

Small appreciation, a "thank you", a touch, an "I see you", a bid for connection; changes the emotional climate. It softens the nervous system. It makes repair possible. This model humbles the egocentricity because it forces self-examination: how often am I noticing what you're doing right versus hunting for what you're doing wrong? Another helpful thing to remember is to always assume the best in your partner rather than assuming the worst. Easier fucking said than done.

The Gottman model isn't about grand gestures. It's about daily, seemingly boring, intentional appreciation that keeps intimacy alive while life and stress are doing their best to kill it.

Esther Perel

Perel pisses people off because she tells the truth most couples avoid: love and desire aren't the same fucking thing, and pretending they are is why so many bedrooms die quietly while everyone stays "nice".

Her work humbles the egocentricity because it shows what happens when we're triggered, insecure, or stuck in routine: we collapse into safety, control, and familiarity. In long-term relationships we want closeness and freedom at the same time, and when we don't understand that tension we blame our partner for what's actually human.

It forces self-examination: how do I kill desire by making you responsible for my worth, my boredom, or my aliveness? It gives couples language to speak honestly about fantasies, needs, distance, and longing without shaming or acting it out sideways. And it brings repair back, not by fixing sex techniques, but by restoring mystery, agency, and choice.

Ian McGilchrist

McGilchrist isn't relationship therapy, but fuck me if it doesn't explain why couples keep missing each other. His whole point is we're dominated by left brain mode: controlling, analysing, categorising, fixing, being fucking certain. When you're triggered, that part takes over and you stop relating, you start managing, correcting, and trying to win.

The right brain stuff, context, emotion, tone, presence, meaning, gets sidelined. So couples argue facts while missing the feeling in the room. His work humbles the egocentricity hard: when you're activated, you're not perceiving reality objectively, you're narrowing it.

It forces the only question that matters: "Am I trying to understand you, or am I trying to be right?". And it points back to the real repair: re-enter relationship instead of debate. Healing and intimacy don't come from better arguments. They come from presence leading instead of control.

These are only a few modalities. I've purposely used different types as examples. There's endless information out there, and you'll probably find one or two that hit you right in the gut and make the rest feel like noise. Good. Use what works.If you can stomach a mix of spiritual practices, along with the science, you will transform. It's not if, it's when.

Everything you've read only matters when shit hits the fan. Not when you're calm. Not when you're nodding along thinking "yeah, that makes sense". It matters in the argument you didn't plan, the silence that lasts too long, the sex that doesn't happen, the moment you feel rejected and something in you snaps. That's where the egocentricity shows up. Shows up to protect us. We aren't little kids anymore. We need to catch it, and defuse the overreaction it's coming with. That's where all this theory either lives or dies.

What comes next isn't inspiration porn or neat examples. It's real life. People fucking this up. Me fucking this up. Couples doing the work badly, clumsily, inconsistently, and still changing because they stopped outsourcing their shit. No miracles. No enlightenment. Just consequences and responsibility. This is where self-work stops being optional and starts being the price of admission for any relationship that doesn't slowly rot from the inside out.

So here's the truth. Nothing in this book will save you. Not the insight. Not the explanations. Not the spiritual bits. Not the psychology. This only works if you stop running, stop blaming, and start catching yourself in real time, when your chest tightens, when the anger rises, when you want to be right, when you want to disappear, when you're about to burn something down instead of staying. That's the work. Not enlightenment. Not perfection. Presence. Ownership. Repair. Again and again and again.

If you do that, your relationships will change. If you don't, you'll keep reading books like this and wondering why the same shit keeps happening with different people. No judgement. No drama. Just cause and effect.

Case Studies

What This Looks Like in Real Life

Carl Jung

"Knowing your own darkness is the best method for dealing with the darkness of other people."

"The meeting of two personalities is like the contact of two chemical substances: if there is any reaction, both are transformed."

James Hollis

"We do not heal in order to become perfect. We heal to become whole."

Viktor Frankl

"When we are no longer able to change a situation, we are challenged to change ourselves."

***

Below are some short clinical case studies, stripped of any real names for confidentiality and anonymity. We say that Anonymity is the Spiritual Foundation in AA.

Case 1

Mark and Elise

Mark and Elise came to couples therapy saying the same thing most couples do: "Our needs aren't being met".

Elise felt unseen, not just by Mark, but as a mother. Their son was ten months old and she was exhausted. Mark felt resentful. He was working two jobs and believed that should earn him space to do whatever the fuck he wanted with the rest of his time.

Over six months, Mark genuinely changed. He showed up more. He tried. In an individual session he finally said what he'd been swallowing: he wanted more affection. Not sex. Affection. Touch. Reassurance.

When he raised it in session, Elise went straight into fight-flight-freeze. She heard pressure. She heard sex. She heard demand. The room was gone. The session imploded. They left worse than they arrived.

Later, Elise booked a solo session. We slowed it down. Unpacked the egocentric hijack. She could see it, not blame herself, but see what happened inside her. They repaired enough to keep going.

That's the work. Not perfection. Repair.

Case 2
Daniel and Brooke

Daniel came to therapy because he couldn't cope with his life without getting out of it. Drinking. Drugs. Night-time escape. Three young kids at home. He didn't want relief, he wanted connection and didn't know it.

There had been violence in the past. Brooke came to a few sessions and wanted none of it. No curiosity. No responsibility. Just blame. When challenged, the door slammed shut. She attacked me, disappeared, and Daniel relapsed.

They both believed the same lie:
If you changed, we'd be fine.

Unless people grow, relationships usually don't survive.

Case 3
Aaron and Jess

Jess came in first. She'd had an emotional affair with a close friend. She swore it never crossed a physical line. Aaron didn't believe her, and honestly, that wasn't the real issue anyway.

Jess stayed. Did the work. Looked at how she'd disconnected long before the affair. Aaron came eventually, dragged in, arms crossed, not interested.

To his credit, once the noise settled, Aaron could actually see his part. Not blame. Responsibility. They weren't guilty, but they were both involved. That gave them a chance to re-build something healthier.

Affairs don't come out of nowhere. They come out of dis-connection.

Case 4
Fred

Fred came in having a full-blown crisis of faith. Lifelong Fundamentalist Christian. Friendships falling apart. Family tension everywhere.

Constant arguments. At the same time, he felt a moral obligation to convince everyone around him of God. Not share. Convince. Pretty quickly it became obvious that the harder he tried to change other people's beliefs, the worse he felt inside.

We talked about the uncomfortable idea that knocking on doors to spread the word of God isn't really about saving anyone else. It's about our own fucking reassurance. If they listen, if they engage, if they don't shut you down com-pletely, if you can convince them, your belief feels stronger. When they reject it, it hits like rejection because it is.

That stung. And he fucking got it.

Fred could finally see why his relationships were getting wrecked. He wasn't connecting. He was regulating his own doubt through other people. The work wasn't about ditch-ing his faith. It was about stopping the unconscious need to recruit others to feel okay inside it.

He didn't lose God. He stopped using people to hold God up for him.

Case 5

Tom and Rachel

Tom was a "nice guy". Raised by a single mum. Learned early that keeping women happy meant staying safe. At first, Rachel loved it. Finally, not another dickhead.

Then the cracks showed. Tom had no backbone. No preferences. No edge.

"What do you want for dinner?"
"Whatever you want, babe."

After a while Rachel didn't feel partnered, she felt like she was parenting. She never wanted kids. Now she felt like she had one.

Tom hated hearing it. His egocentricity fought hard. But he did the work. Read "No More Mr Nice Guy". Sat with the discomfort. Kept going.

I still see them occasionally. Completely different relationship.

Case 6
Luke and Hannah

Blended family. Five kids between them. Luke assumed Hannah would just "handle it". Pub nights. Money blown from the joint account. Zero awareness.

Hannah was furious, and rightfully so. She remembered the man Luke pretended to be at the start. I tried with Luke. He couldn't see past blame. Wouldn't own his shit. The relationship ended.

Hannah stayed in therapy for a year. Looked at why she chose him. She's now with a balanced partner who's also in therapy.

That's not coincidence. If only one person grows, the relationship always has an end date.

Case 7
Steve

Steve came in raging. His wife had an affair. Real estate agent. Arrogant. Angry at everyone: her, the kids, his boss, the roadwork guy holding the STOP sign.

He wanted a venting booth. He called his wife a slut so often I stopped hearing her name. I tried gently. Nothing landed. His egocentricity was armoured.

One day, right at the start of the session as he walked in, I leaned forward and said:
"So... how's the slut today?" Silence. Shock. Egocentricity cracked.

That wasn't textbook. That was timing. A cold slap with a wet fish. It could've gone badly. It didn't. He woke up, just enough.

I still see Steve. His wife comes now too. They both take responsibility. They're adjusting. Repairing.

Not every approach is pretty. But sometimes it works.

Case 8
Craig & Vanessa

Craig and Vanessa met online and fell hard, fast. Deep connection straight out of the gate. No slow burn, no buffer.

With that speed, they hit the trauma layers early, too early. Old wounds got activated before there was enough safety. It ruptured things quickly and could've ended it just as fast.

Instead, they both stayed. Not clung, stayed. Took responsibility. Did the work individually, not just together. Learned how to slow it down, regulate, and build safety after the explosion.

They're still together over three years later.
Fast love doesn't doom a relationship.
Unconscious speed does.

Case 9
Phil

Phil came in abusive, arrogant, dismissive. Treated me the way he treated his wife. I tried to get through to him, the only thing speaking to me throughout the session was his egocentricity.

I told him straight, I wasn't the therapist for him.
Phil left offended. Smug. Certain he was smarter than me.
I felt for his wife. His kids. His colleagues.

We don't all get well.

Sometimes It's Not You

Violence, Control, and the Line That Can't Be Crossed

Let's be very clear about something before anyone twists this book into a justification for being a cunt. Or thinks I'm condoning any type of abusive actions. Understanding behaviour is not excusing it. When we are talking about violence or abuse, it's definitely not you, and always them. What you can do is notice any patterns in the relationships you choose. That part is you.

Domestic violence and coercive control are not "relationship issues". They are power issues. They are fear issues. Hitting, threatening, isolating, monitoring, intimidating, controlling money, controlling movement, controlling who someone sees or speaks to — that is not love gone wrong. That is dominance. And dominance is the egocentricity in its most dangerous form.

Yes, these behaviours come from insecurity.
Yes, they come from fear.
Yes, they come from a nervous system that learned control equals safety.

But none of that makes it acceptable. People are responsible for their actions 100% of the time when it come to abuse or violence.

This book explains why people get triggered, defensive, avoidant, or reactive. It does not excuse harming others. Once violence or coercive control enters a relationship, the priority is safety — not insight, not repair, not couples work, not "understanding each other better".

If you are being harmed, your job is not to be patient, compassionate, or more self-aware.

Your job is to get safe.

If you are the one using control, intimidation, or violence, insight alone won't save you. Understanding your childhood, your trauma, or your attachment style does not undo the damage. Responsibility starts with stopping the behaviour, accepting consequences, and getting serious help — not asking for empathy while others live in fear.

This book is about consciousness.

Violence is unconsciousness with a body count.

If you are experiencing abuse or domestic violence, help is available. A good place to start is to phone 1800RESPECT.

Final Word

This book has already done the explaining.

If it rattled you, pissed you off, or made you see yourself a bit clearer, good. That means it did something good, that means it achieved what I set out to do. A line out of my favourite book states "whenever I am disturbed, the problem is with me".

The problem is clear.
The patterns are clear.
The escapes are clear.
The path is clear.

Healthy relationships are not complicated. They are just uncomfortable.

Stay present instead of escaping.
Take responsibility instead of blaming.
Repair instead of defending.

Do that and relationships change.
Don't and they don't.

Contact

For professional enquiries, speaking, retreats, or clinical work:

Whatsapp:
+61 432 631 992

Website:
www.chadtaylorpsychotherapy.com.au

Email:
chadtaylorpsychotherapy@gmail.com

Podcast:
Conversations for Conscious Relationships

Podcast:
Between Us: Therapists in Relationship

If this book landed for
you and gave you something
real, an honest review
helps more than you think.
Not a five-star performance
— just the truth.

If it felt like a waste
of time, or you honestly
got fuck all out of it,
email me and I'll refund
the purchase price. No
arguments. No defensive
emails. No bullshit.

All I ask is this: don't throw
it in the bin. Leave it
somewhere public — a cafe, a
park bench, a waiting room —
and let it find someone it
might actually help.
Not everything's for everyone.
Till next time,
Chad

www.ingramcontent.com/pod-product-compliance
Lightning Source LLC
Chambersburg PA
CBHW051258020426
42333CB00026B/3265